THE

MYSTERIES AND MISERIES

OF

New York:

•

A STORY OF REAL LIFE,

By NED BUNTLINE

~~~~~~~~~

PART I

NEW YORK

EDWARD Z C JUDSON

1848

DEDICATION

—

TO THE REVEREND CLERGY OF NEW YORK

THIS WORK IS RESPECTFULLY INSCRIBED WITH A FERVENT

HOPE THAT THEY MAY SEE AND REMEDY

THE EVILS WHICH IT

DESCRIBES

PREFATORIAL

As a general thing I dislike prefatory remarks but so singular is the work I have now to write so strange its scenes and incidents so various and peculiar the characters which I have to delineate that I feel bound to te l the reader that strange as all may be it is drawn from *life* heart-sickening *too real* life   Not one scene of vice or horror is given in the following pages which has not been enacted over and over again in this city nor is there one character which has not its counterpait in our very midst   I have sought out and studied the re ality of each person and scene which I portray   Accompanied Ly several kind and efficient police officers whom were it proper I would gratefully name I have visited every den of vice which is hereinafter described and have chosen each character for this work during these visits   Therefore though this book bears the title of a *novel* it is writ ten with the ink of truth and deserves the name of a *history* more than that of a *romance*

Should *christians* those good and devout people who supply the sun scorched Hottentots with woollen blankets and the fishing Indians of the barren isles of the southern seas with agricultural implements and send their missionaries there at an expense of millions to convert them to our ways should these people for whom I entertain no disrespect, shudder at pictures which they see in the following chapters (if they ever condescend to read the *novel*) I pray them to seek out the spots which I describe and see for themselves whether missionaries are not *more* needed here   aye in the very centre of this great city than in the far off lands of India or the isles of the South where the heathen are *children* in vice and degradation when compared to the heathen among us   I mean no slur upon the noble and good missionary cause—the best of our land have engaged in it heart and hand—one of its chiefs is a kin in name* and blood to the writer but I do say that missiona

* N d Bun   is a *nomm du plum* —Edw rd Z C Jud o is the writer s real nam

ries can find a darker deeper field for labor in New York than they can in any savage land

I know that this work will offend many persons for it will strike at vice in every garb and station, the gambling *palaces* of Gotham shall have their place in my chapters as well as the less fashionable dens of infamy where the thieves and beggars most do congregate I write for the good of my fellow mortals and shall do it with a bold truthful fearless hand aiming to do my *whole duty* regardless of all consequences Let the following pages be my test

In regard to my dedication I have now a few words to say to the Clergy of the City of New York

REVEREND GENTLEMEN

Do not think that I mean any insult by inscribing as I have to you a professed *novel* do not think that I lack in respect for your glorious and holy calling ,—though no zealot though not filled with any sectarian bigotry I respect and love the *true* minister of God wherever I find him let his doctrinal opinions be as they may

I inscribe this work to you because I wish it to be read by you and by those who have the benefit of your instructions for though it wears the cloak of a romance it is full to overflowing of painful truths which are but too glaringly displayed here in our very midst I have striven to write a work which in point of morality shall be unobjectionable one which you can lay before your wives and daughters to read and from which they may take lessons that will learn them to be thankful that they are comfortable pure and happy even in a city where such dreadful contrasts of misery vice and utter degradation can be found

Read but this extract from one of your municipal documents the report of the City Alms House Commissioners for the last year After enumerating the crowded hospitals the various asylums for the destitute full to overflowing they allude to the out-door poor and say

Destitution is found in every street—families of nearly all nations occupying the rudest hovels and lowest cellars all filled to repletion —children of every age clustering around their parents asking for food and fire with scarcely a comfort or convenience to render their abodes an apology for a home most of them with nothing to do to earn any money many of them suffering in sickness and all presenting so dire a picture of extreme poverty that no language can describe it "

This Reverend Gentlemen is the ground work upon which I found this romance—many a weary day many a dreary sickening night have I spent in the search for its material and I have seen persons and scenes which *indeed* I cannot find language to describe

I have an aim in this work—it is to do good   I wish to lay before you all the vice of the city to lay open its festering sores so that you and the good and philanthropic may see where to apply the healing balm , I wish to show where and how our young men are led away and ruined in the glittering gambling palaces , how manv a poor now , wretched and degraded female has been driven into the paths of infamy by neglect when one kind word and one helping hand would have saved her

This work is written for Christians to read therefore Gentlemen I have dedicated it to you   And if you read it in the cold winter evenings which even now are close at hand I pray you to remember and pity those who know not the privileges and comforts which you enjoy who are morally and physically dying around you all the time

No   —A glossary explaining al of the slang and flash terms used in the work will be found appended

MYSTERIES AND MISERIES OF NEW YORK.

CHAPTER I

NOT in the olden time when the people differed as much from us in character as in costume, do we commence this story—but now, in modern days, when every man, woman, and child, who reads it, can recognise its characters and descriptions

On the first day of January, eighteen hundred and forty one, it rained cold rain and the winds blew strong and gustily in New York, and as the night came on, it grew colder and colder until the falling rain became sleet and the wind freshened into a gale The day closed thus, and the bright street lamps were lighted Then could be seen the miserable street walkers taking their nightly round up and down Broadway, poor, painted, tinseled creatures, now pausing before the large windowed hotels to show themselves to the cigar smoking loungers who occupied the big arm chairs within, then smiling with a faint and sickly smile upon some country looking promenader, thus throwing out a bait to induce him to turn aside at the next street corner to speak to them, or to make him follow them to the theatre of their nightly infamy   And they shivered as they went along, for some were very thinly dressed , their powdered necks and swelling bo soms were not half covered, and even those who were better dressed, who had muffs and boas and velvet cloaks, felt the pierc ing wind which shrilly whistled through the leafless branches of the Park trees, and blew the sharp sleet into their unveiled faces Of all the Broadway promenaders at that hour, these miserable females were in number predominant, for few were abroad who were not forced out from NECESSITY, that lawless fiend who asks all and gives nothing

And even amidst these, as a lily among nettles, or a dove among vultures, passed one of their own sex who was pure , one yet undarkened with the taint which for ever clouds an erring wo man's fame   She was a young girl—a glance at her large blue eyes, golden hair and *petite* figure, as she passed beneath the lighted lamps, would tell one that she was not over sixteen, but her young face seemed thin with care, her large eyes were sad and mournful in expression   So far as her garb could be seen— it was neat, though of very common material and she seemed very thinly dressed—although a coarse woolen shawl was wrap ped around her, beneath which she carried a large bundle

Her steps were rapid and she trembled as she hurried along, for she heard rude and uncouth sounds, and she shuddered as she met the depraved beings of her own sex, who stared each man rudely in the face who passed them   And she shrank aside when she saw groups of young men come reeling and laughing along, young men who had just got up from their wine dinners, and the timid one would draw closer the front of her black hood as she saw them rudely stare at her

And thus had she passed the gauntlet until she reached the vi cinity of Park Place, where two huge, parti colored lamps, inform the passer by that ' Florence " is in New York, and she had passed so far free from insult   But here a party of young men, who had just come from a certain *No three* in the immediate vi cinity, where liquor and suppers can be had *gratis* by the *initiated*, saw how timidly she hurried along the outer side of the pavement, and as if by general consent stepped before her so that she could not pass

" Ha ! my little dove, where are you flying to at this time o' night ?" cried one of them, while another took the answer upon himself, and replied

" To her nest to be sure ! Don't you want company, my little chick ?"

The poor creature trembled and seemed as if she would sink to the earth—she looked around as if to seek aid or see whither to fly, but now they had completely encircled her

" Please let me go, gentlemen—I am not what you take me for ! Oh, do let me hurry home—my poor mother is waiting for me !'" murmured she in a supplicating tone

" Then your mother knows you're out?" cried the first speaker, and while he rudely turned her face so that the lamp light could shine upon it, he added—" I'll have to see you home, my lady bird—by Jove, but you're a Venus, only you are a little minus in the filling up—you have to work, I reckon?"

" Oh, yes, sir, but do let me go—I am carrying home work now, and I must not, cannot stay!"

" What, a little sewing girl, eh? The very game I like—go away, boys, and let me talk to her—I spoke to her first, and by Jupiter, I'm the one to see it out!"

" No—not quite so rapid, if you please," replied the one who had spoken second—" we'll toss up, Harry, who shall have her!"

" Oh! Heavens, gentlemen, *do* let me go I am not what you take me for!" cried the poor creature, and now great tears ran down her blushing cheeks These were fashionable young *gentlemen*, sons of the " first families," and yet they saw those tears —saw her clasp her thin hands in supplication, and felt no pity— stayed not their cruel persecution, and to her last beseeching expression, only replied with a scornful laugh, while he who had been addressed as Harry put his hand in his pocket, and cried to the other

" Yes, I'll toss up for her, Gus! Here goes!" and up flew a silver dollar in the air, down came the same with a clear ring up on the sleety pavement, while Gus, who had shouted " *head* " as it went up, bent down to find it

" *Tail,* by Jove!" he muttered, with a bitter curse, as he raised the dollar and handed it back to the other

" Then I win, and here, my girl, is the dollar to commence on!" cried Harry

The girl did not take the coin—her tears seemed at once to dry on her cheeks, and young as she was, there was a queenly dignity in both tone and manner, as she cried

" I take no money, sir, but that which I earn by honest labor! Once more I demand a passage among you I *will* go home!"

" Not so fast, my beauty! You're mine now, I've won a right to you I shall go home, or somewhere else with you!"

" God protect me!" murmured the girl, then with a kind of desperate firmness in her manner, she pressed forward to try to force her way from amongst the crowd of drunken libertines

But he who had won in the toss up, clasped her firmly in his arms, in vain she tried to spring from his grasp   Then she uttered a wild, piercing cry—a shriek of terror and agony   And it was not in vain, for the next moment a tall form stood among the laughing young men, two or three heavy blows were *heard* and felt rather than seen, and with each blow one of the party laid down   Before Harry could turn to see who it was that interfered, a large bony hand reached his cheek, and though struck by its open palm, he let go of the poor girl and staggered up against the lamp post

"Big Lize, of Thomas street!" he muttered, as he saw the tall form of the one who had struck him and his companions

"Yes, I am Big Lize, you lushy swell!" cried the woman, "and I can maul every sneaking mother's son of ye!   What d'ye mean by stoppin' this ere gal against her will?"

"It's none of your business, go look out for yourself, you thieving catamaran!" cried the young man, recovering somewhat from the stunning effects of the blow, and again springing toward the poor sewing girl, who shrank behind the huge form of her protectress

"You will have it then, my covey   you're mighty fond of my *mawley!*" cried Big Lize, as with another blow, she landed him clear down the stairs of the oyster saloon, which was behind him, and then turning to the girl, she cried, "Cut and run, my darling!   Hays is the word, and off you go!   I'll see that they don't follow you!"

Then, when the poor girl, with one glad expression, "God bless you!" on her lips, fled up the street, Big Lize turned and again confronted the party, none of whom dared to stir after the girl whom she had rescued   Lize stood and gazed at them a moment, while upon her dissipation marked, but yet firm features, a freezing expression of scorn and contempt settled, then as she turned away and walked up the street, that expression gave way to one of deep sadness, mingled apparently with a satisfaction at the act which she had just performed

"God bless me!" she murmured, repeating the last, grateful words of the poor girl whom she had protected   "Yes, I have need of such prayers, for God, or man, or the devil, or all together, seem to have cursed me!   Oh God!   I once wore the stamp of nnocence on my brow—once I rode along these very streets in my father's carriage, and now"——

"Hallo, old gal, where are you stavin' to? Have you lifted anything to night?"

The speaker who thus interrupted Lize in her soliloquy was a short, well dressed, fine looking little fellow, with a pair of keen black eyes, and seemed to be a friend well known to her, for, stretching out her hand, she replied—

"How d'ye, Charley, my chum! I haven't lifted nuthin' as yet, but I mauled some o' the bigbug swells a bit ago. If you'd a been there you might have larnt 'em some lessons in the knucking line?"

"What, warn't none of the files on the tramp?"

"Not a mammy's son of 'em!"

"What did you maul the swells for?"

"'Cause they were abusin' a gal—a poor bit of a thing that hasn't got hell's mark on her yet—that's innocent as I was ten years ago!"

"You might have been in better business, Lize. You're too blasted good hearted to be on the tramp, but stir your pegs, old gal, I'm agoin' to the crib, see if you can't pick up some cove as wants to see the elephant!"

"Wall, tramp along, chummy," replied the girl, "I'll see what's what, my chuck!"

And then the girl sighed, when she found herself alone again, and pulled her shawl closer around her. She was a very singular looking woman. No doubt many of my readers have seen her as she has passed to and fro on the Broadway tide if so, they will recognise this description

Very tall, nearly or quite six feet in height, a form well proportioned, a carriage rather graceful, features that once must have been remarkably handsome, and even yet are fine and regular, though the hollow cheek, and high cheek bones, and narrowing chin, denote the havoc of time and dissipation, a large, piercing eye of hazel, lips which now are thin and close, set over white and regular teeth—lips which have firmness written in their expression, a high brow, upon which crescent shaped and delicately pencilled eye brows are seen, dark hair, even yet soft and glossy, though thinned and shortened See this—and fancy a touch of paint on either cheek and a coat of powder on a rather slim neck and broad uncovered shoulders, and "Big Lize, of Thomas street," is before you

We will leave her to seek a victim for her panel crib, for she has long been an active panel thief, while we follow the poor little sewing girl

Up Broadway until she has reached Canal street, then down that broad thoroughfare toward the North River she fled, swiftly, though her weak limbs tottered and trembled under her, never pausing, though she was panting and almost breathless, until she reached a street leading diagonally with that down which she hurried Into this she turned, and soon from it passed into a narrow little alley way -a filthy, sickening place—along which stretched a row of low, old frame houses, each looking as if they would crumble and fall down if they only had room to do so

Into one of these, or rather its cellar, she stepped, and, as she pushed open the creaking old door, fell forward upon the bare ground and fainted Terror and exhaustion had done the work She lay senseless upon the ground, while the bundle, to which she had clung all this time, rolled out from under her arm

" My poor child -poor Angelina ! what is the matter ?" cried a pale, sickly looking woman, who, when the girl entered, had been seated at the farther corner of the cellar, sewing by the light of a small tallow dip, which stood on the head of a barrel, the only table visible in the dark, cheerless hole

But the girl answered not she lay still, even as if the hand of death was upon her With trembling haste the mother—for this was indeed that poor girl's widowed mother—seized the light, and kneeling by her daughter's side, raised her head on one arm, while she gazed tearfully down upon her face

" No—not dead !—she breathes—she has fainted !" murmured the woman , and then setting down the candle, she raised the poor girl's form and bore it to a little cot bed which stood near her work table This was the neatest spot in the cellar, for a piece of old rag carpet was placed before it, and the blanket that covered the bed, though threadbare, was clean By the rustle that the bed made when the woman laid her daughter upon it, could be discovered its material—straw Ah, how many in this city have not even *that* to lay down upon !

When she had laid her daughter down, she hurried to where a broken pitcher stood beside her " work table," and, returning, commenced bathing the poor girl's face and brow with its con tents, and tried to pour some between her lips The water seemed to have effect, for in a few moments the girl slowly opened her eyes, then with a shudder closed them again, while she slowly passed her hand across them, as if to wipe away the remembrance of some horrible vision

" It is me, my daughter ' Oh, what is the matter ' Poor— poor child—you are so weak and so tired'"

" They did not follow ' I am safe , but I ran so fast '" mur mured the girl faintly , and her thin form shook with the shudder that passed over her frame

" What do you mean, my poor girl , have you been in danger? Oh God ' has harm come to thee, my child ?"

The girl raised herself partly up on her elbow Her eye did not wander now so wildly as before, and she seemed to regain a knowledge of where she was

" My dear—dear mother '" she cried , and then as she threw her thin arms around the neck of her parent, the poor girl wept— wept for very joy that she was now safe And then, while she yet was sobbing, in broken accents she told her mother of the scene which we have already described—how she had been insulted by things wearing the garb of *men*—how a terrible woman had rushed in and rescued her, and, with stre ⸢⸣ anguage but kind looks, bade her go home—and ho ⸢⸣ne had ran all the way, over a mile, amid the pelting bla , and never let go of the bundle which con tained work for nerself and her mother

And then, after her tale was told, she shivered and said—

"I am very cold, mother '"

" Yes, poor child, I know you are Your thin hands feel like marble in my grasp , but you have brought money, we will buy wood and have a fire , and then I know you're hungry, poor thing, you've only eaten one potatoe to day '"

" I am not hungry, mother , but I've brought no money '"

" No money, child ' Have we worked night and day for a whole week to be disappointed in our pay ' Why did they not give it you ?"

" They told me to come in the morning, mother , and when I

begged them to give it me to-night, they got angry, and spoke so harsh, and said that you could trust them for a paltry two dollars —and then I took the new bundle of work which was cut out, and came away' We can wait till morning, mother "

" Yes, and you freezing, starving, dying, my poor child ! Oh God, is not poverty a crime ! Why, why are we cursed with it !"

" Don't fret, dear mother I'll get within the bed, and when you come too, we'll put our clothes on over the blanket and we'll soon get warm , for you will press me to your bosom, and say kind words, as you ever do That will soon warm my heart There are others poorer than we !"

" Oh no child , it is impossible ! When that candle is burned out, I have not one cent to buy another !"

" But I will go in the morning and get the week's earnings The two dollars will make us comfortable again , and then we can make two more, if we work hard "

" Alas ! my child , I fear our strength cannot hold out to keep us up during the long, terrible winter They tell a sad tale of those who lived here last winter, you know ! '

" Yes, mother, I have heard them say that they burned up the floor for firewood, and that even then it did not save them, for when morning came after a cold, bitter night at the dead of win ter, the parents found their two little children dead But, mother, they were drunkards, you know, and they cared but little for their poor babies !"

" Too true, my child , and God ca~d for the poor creatures by taking them out of a world so cold—so wicked as this Some times-I wish that you—you whom I so fondly love, my child— had died ere want and woe came upon us !"

" And then, dear mother, you would have been left to struggle alone Oh no ! thank God that I have been spared to aid you But you shiver, you, too, are cold, come to bed and sleep till the morrow, and then I will go and get the money, and we will have fire and food I love to sleep, for I almost always dream of happy days that are past, and sometimes dream of joys that are to come, which makes me glad until I wake "

We have other scenes to go to, reader This we will leave for the present

CHAPTER II

———

'Curse that infernal girl! I believe she has blacked both of my eyes She hits harder than Bill Lord ever did, and he has laid me out twice in the same way, and for about the same thing," muttered Henry Whitmore, as he "picked himself up" after Big Lize had "landed" him at the foot of Florence's steps

His companions at once gathered around him, and his particu lar friend, Gustave Livingston, who had *lost* when they tossed up for the possession of the poor sewing girl, now bantered him, crying in a gay tone—

"You got more than was up in the bill, eh, Harry! I'm glad I didn't win in the toss up!"

"Blast the luck! But where's the girl?"

"Big Lize, do you mean?"

"No—confound it, no! The little beauty—the sewing girl"

"Oh, she's off long ago, and has got Lize to protect her at that You're *knocked* out of your chance this time!" jeered Gustave And then, as if to make amends for his rather untimely joke, he added, "let's walk up to the bar and enter a plea, boys, I've had my fun, and it's my treat'

As this was an invitation which fashionable young gentlemen never decline, Florence at once became the price of nine drinks the richer, and the young gentlemen had another tier of grog in their spirit rooms

Then Harry, who could not recover his spirits, even though his glass had been filled with some of that B B B, the black bottled best, proposed that they should take a round"

"Where shall we go?" asked Gustave

' Why I've had bad luck in at number three—s'pose we try our fortune up at Pat Hisen's He does things up in style—keeps the best liquors, and sets the best supper table in town"

"You're right He's a gentleman, every inch of him, and be
2

sides, his company is very select   You'll always find more army
and navy officers there than anywhere else in town   I heard a
right good thing from him about that the other day

"What was it?" cried all the party

Why, one of the army boys, —— ——, one that distinguished
himself and came confounded near getting extinguished out in the
Florida war, went in with some friends, and after partaking of a
most magnificent supper, walked up to Pat to apologise for not
going to the faro table to play, saying that he never *gamed* "

"Don't apologize, my dear sir—don't say a word!" replied
Pat, in that broad, rich tone of his   "I'm always glad to see
you and your friends here   Even if you don't play, your presence
gives a *tone* to the establishment   I'm glad, I 'asshure' you, to
see you here "

" And, no doubt, he was   Well, Pat is the man for my money,
or I for his, to night!" cried Harry Whitmore, and ascending to
the *pavé*, the young men wrapped their cloaks closely around
them, and proceeded up Broadway, now stopping to pass some
coarse jest with a poor street walker, then breaking out in some
bacchanalian song with a full chorus

On they staggered up the street, across Canal, passing all until
they came to the neighborhood of the renowned NIBLO's, where,
crossing the street, they found themselves at the door of what
appeared to be a very genteel private residence   No name was
on the door, yet the number—five hundred, and I forget the lesser
numbers—was graven on a neat plate

Harry rang the bell, and it was answered in a moment by a
very neatly dressed and genteel servant, who, without a word,
admitted the party within the first door, but another was before
them, through which they could not pass without the knowledge
and consent of the master of the establishment   But they had not
long to wait in the corridor—the card of Harry was sent up, and
the consequence was a polite invitation to walk up   Up a neatly
carpeted stair case to the second story they passed, where the door
was opened into a splendid back parlor   Here they were met by
Mr Hisen *in propria persona*   He had one of those bland, ever
smiling faces which so well becomes a man of the world, an eye
at once quick and searching in its glances, and features that would
form quite a map of study for a physiognomist

He was well dressed, yet the flashiness of the sporting man, " stuck out " a little There was a very slight mellowness in his voice, as he welcomed the party, which bore a shade of *the* brogue in it, but not enough to make one think him a late impor tation from the Green Isle of the sea

" Glad to see you, gentlemen ! rather early, but I'm glad to see you, nevertheless ! It's coolish out to night I was just thinking of brewing a bowl of " the real mountain dew," hot, or if either of you prefer, there's some " 1801 brandy " on the side board , very rare old stuff, been bottled for twelve years to my own knowledge , walk up and make yourselves perfectly at home !"

It was remarkable how very fast the neat little gentleman could talk , the words, too, came with a liquid flow from his lips, with a kind of unstudied persuasiveness which made it impossible for those who were present to refuse his invitation

Therefore, the punch was brewed, we need not add that it was drank, and then cigars were introduced, for as Mr H had re marked, it was " rather early," too early for a fashionable game, and none but *fashionable* men ever visited that establishment The room in which they sat was furnished in a neat and tasty style of elegance, two or three very fine landscapes were hung upon the walls, but none of those glaring, lascivious paintings, which in a lower order of gambling hells are always to be seen The side boards were well set off with a handsome display of cut glass decanters, &c , which of course were all filled with the choicest wines and liquors , a centre table was covered with the best papers and periodicals of the day among which the " tall Son of York's " excellent " Spirit, ' the *old* " Knickerbocker," " Albion," &c , were to be seen Everything here was rich, neat and tasty There was a front parlor, too, but we will take a peep into that by and by, when the ball commences

The party smoked and drank , others came in, and time went on until the hour of eleven Then came a change over the scene The centre table was moved aside, a long supper table was set and soon loaded with all that a gourmand could wish for, even with the best which the market could produce And when the guests were seated—pop ! pop ! went the champaigne corks—the more heavy and serious sherry and Madeira was quietly poured out with its gurgle, gurgle, so like the eddying brooklet, and some, of superior taste to all, saw their glasses filled with the "London brown S," its saffron colored foam o'ermantling the dark clear essence of the malt beneath

But even these enjoyments, like all others, were fleeting, the supper was over , midnight was at hand, and it was time for more *fashionable* amusements

The party arose from the table , the wide folding doors which separated them from the next room were thrown open, and they entered an apartment furnished full as neatly as the other, but with one article in it which we have not seen before   It is a long table—a rich heavy one of carved and polished mahogany, and upon one end of it are piled heaps of red and white ivory checks, things which are changed for money, used for the same in betting, and are redeemable for cash at the bank—the *faro* bank we mean

A little silver box stands upon the centre of the table, and in front of this box is arranged a suit of cards, face up, on the table, and within the box is another set similar to them   We forgot to say that behind this box stands a most elegant looking gentle man , a tall, slim, middle aged gentleman, who smiles as the par ty enter, and looks as if butter never could melt in his mouth

And now the party gather in front of the table, while Mr H seats himself on the right hand of the dealer to attend to the du ties of banker   He opens the little casket which is to contain the evening's *earnings*, or winnings, to call them rightly, and with a *winning* smile, cries,

" Proceed, gentlemen , we are all ready now for a quiet little game   Make your bets "

And he is obeyed

" Give me checks for a twenty, Pat !" cries Harry Whitmore, throwing down a bank bill of the XX size

The round pieces of ivory are in his hand, and then others get their bills changed in a similar way   The dealer shuffles his cards, slips them into his box, and again Pat's rich voice is heard

" Make your bets, gentlemen , the board is open "

Down goes ten dollars of Harry W 's money on a king , others bet on different cards, and then the dealer slips off the cards, first one to the right, and then one to the left   Ere another card is touch ed the bets are attended to Those that have lost, see their money raked into the heap before the banker, and the few that win receive their checks All again make their bets and so on until the deal is out

Harry Whitmore was in luck, he kept winning until he had more than made up his losses at number *three* Park Place, but others were at that fatal board whom fortune favored not so much There was a tall, fine looking young fellow, who had played with great boldness, but with constant loss from the time the bank opened

"Who is he?" asked Gus Livingston of his friend Harry

"Not knowing, can't say," replied Harry, but at the same time he propounded the question to a "sporting *gentleman*" who was apparently only "a looker on in Vienna," but who really was a "look out' in the employ of the bank, who, stationed outside the table as a common spectator, could aid the bank much by timely suggestions to "green 'uns" and also could see that the betters only took up their winnings

To Harry s question in regard to the young man who played so desperately and lost so largely, the "look out" replied

"He is a clerk with S———, the dry goods man, sir?"

"Is he wealthy?"

"I don't know, he makes a pretty fair show Shall I intro duce you?'

"Yes, by all means He is a fellow of spirit, I like to see a man play deep'"

"So do I,' replied the sporting gentleman, and then he added *sotto voce* "especially when he has charge of the key of his employer's iron chest'"

Of course, this last remark was not heard, and while the dealer shuffled the pack for a fresh deal, Harry and his party were intro duced in due form to Mr Charles Meadows

'You seem out of luck to night, sir'" said Harry to him, af ter the usual salutations had passed

"Yes, I've cursed bad luck I've lost three thousand to night and lost two last night'"

"You play deep'"

"Yes, but luck must change you know, it can't always keep on in this way'"

The gambler who had introduced him heard this remark, and with a low chuckle, said again in an under tone

"It'll last till you drain the old man's chest, or are found out, my hearty!" but of course the remark reached not the ears of the young men

"The game's set, gentlemen! Make your bets!" again was heard from the dealer, and once more Mr H put on one of those inviting smiles

"Try your luck once more, Mr Meadows?" said he—"your turn must come soon, Fortune's wheel is ever revolving?"

"It's a devilish long time in getting round to the right point for me," replied the young man, and then as he glanced down at the pretty cards which lay upon the table, he added—"I've got just a hundred left, I'll lay it all on the ace!"

This was done, other bets were made and the deal commenced

"Curse the luck!" cried Meadows, as his ace lost, while his eyes flashed with excitement, "I say, Pat, won't you lend me fifty?"

"I'm the very worst man in the world to borrow money of, my dear sir, upon my honor, but just step into the back room and tell Duane to give it to you I'll endorse your I O U"

The fifty was soon received, and almost as quickly lost Mea dows grew pale when he saw it go, but he tried to smile, and turned away, saying

"It's of no use for me to play to night I'll wait till to morrow evening"

Then he strode to the side board, filled a tumbler half full of raw brandy, emptied it at a swallow, after which he bade the party good evening and left the room

"Do you know where he boards? By Jove! he is a man of spirit, I must get acquainted with him!" said Harry Whitmore, addressing himself to the gambler—(we beg his pardon, sporting gentleman, we mean)—who was on the look out

"I don't know, sir I only meet him here, you will find him here almost every night As I said before, he is one of the head clerks of S———, the dry goods merchant, a confidential clerk at that!"

"S——— don't know of his coming here, does he?'

' I should think not, sir, nor do I think Charley Meadows

would like S——— to know it   These mercantile men will ne
ver let their clerks gamble at cards, though they themselves gam
ble in the rise and fall of their stock "

We will leave this party now for a little while, and follow
young Meadows from this elegant and *recherché* establishment

When he reached the door, and felt the cold gale strike his burn
ing forehead, he raised the hat which he had drawn down over
his eyes, and as he passed down the now silent street, he mut
tered

" One more night of sin !   I am now ten thousand dollars out,
and if S——— were to discover it, disgrace and ruin would be
mine   Oh, God ! this is too bad !   I have robbed my employer,
stolen from one who has heaped me with kindnesses, who has
enabled me for years to support my poor mother and dear sister,
But I will repay it and quit for ever   One lucky night and I can
regain all and replace it !   I was lucky at first, everybody says
they play a fair game up there, but it is strange that I can always
win on *small* bets and lose on *large* ones "

The young man turned from Broadway down a street not far
from Canal, and after walking a short distance, paused at the door
of a neat little brick house   As he paused, he heard the iron
tongues of the different city bells strike two, and after feeling in
his pocket a moment, he muttered again

" It is too bad, I've lost my night key somewhere, I shall have
to ring and wake the old lady up "

He touched the knob of the bell wire, and while the bell was
yet tingling, the door was opened

" What, mother ! are you up yet ?" he asked of a thin, pale,
but sweet-looking lady, who might, by her appearance, be forty
five, certainly not more   She was dressed in deep mourning

" Yes, Charles, Isabella and myself could not sleep when we
knew you were at work over your books   What a dreadful night
it is out !"

" Yes , it is bleak and dreary, mother, but you should not have
waited for me , I told you that I had so many accounts to make
out, that I couldn't get home early !"

" Poor boy, you have to work so hard , Mr S——— surely will
raise your salary this winter   We have hard work to get on
and educate Isabella on eight hundred a year "

"Yes, it is true, mother!" and the young man sighed as he took off his cloak and hat

Was that sigh caused by the recollection that he had lost thir ty one hundred and fifty dollars that very night?

He followed his mother into the neat but plainly furnished little back parlor, and as he crossed the threshold, his sister arose from her seat beside the centre table, where she had been read ing, and with a glad smile hurried to meet him, and pressed her pure warm lips to his with a kiss such as a *sister* only can give

Reader will you pardon a digression What on all the earth is purer, truer, firmer than a sister's love She loves as woman, yet not with passion, not as others love, only when love is return ed Oh, who that has possessed a sister can ever forget her first fond affection, her warm, holy, passionless kiss The writer has one, and though years have gone by since fate has separated him from her, never, never can he forget the fond hours of their childhood's love, though now time and distance and the love of another may have estranged her, yet will the memory of their in fant hours bring back to him, joy, love and gladness, linked with the name of his only sister, IRENE

And Charles Meadows returned his fond sister's kiss, yes, wi h lips which had breathed curses but an half hour before, and had opened to the burning draught which he had taken to stifle con-science

Isabella Meadows was beautiful! Dressed in an evening *ne glege*, neat but plain, she looked as pure as an angel Her eyes were of a dark hazel, so nearly black that by candle light it would seem they were so In dark brown curls her hair fell upon a snow white neck, which with its graceful curves would have served Canova for a model, her form was tall, slender, yet perfectly proportioned, and if, as sculptors say, the foot and limbs may be judged by the sight of the hand, her small, delicate, taper ed hand, would pronounce hers to be perfection She seemed to be about sixteen, and each word from her lips, each look and ac tion, showed her to be a child of nature

We will now leave this scene, but the reader need not fear to lose sight of any scene or character that has been laid before him We will follow all through their varying life cruise, and trace each character to its end

CHAPTER III

ANOTHER day has passed in our history—a cold, tempestuous day of winter Oh, what suffering had been felt on that day—how many a starving, dying wretch had felt the keen biting of the frost, with no fire to warm the cold limbs and the colder heart,—no friend to speak the kind word of sympathy—no Christian to tell them that repentance and faith might lead them to a home in another world where the sorrows and ills of this would be all for gotten Thousands have thus died—men and women who have been nursed in the very hot beds of infamy and vice, here in this great city, who have never heard the names of our Holy God or of his precious Son, save as they were shouted in oaths and blas phemy This is not romance, reader—it is but *too* true !

Another day has passed and once more we will look within the cellar of the poor sewing girl and her mother It is not quite so drear and desolate as when last we left them, for though it is dark and dreary outside, they have a candle upon the old barrel head, and a little fire in the hearth place The two dollars have evi dently been received, and they are now more comfortable But the light of their fire and candle serve only to show how very poor they are The bare, rough, cracked stone walls, the un floored earth, two low stools, the barrel table, the little cot bed stead, alone are seen

The mother and daughter are at work, see them with their thin fingers stitching away over the garments for which they are paid so little, the garments which will be worn with pride where the rich and beautiful are assembled Steadily they work, for time to them is too precious to be wasted—each moment is as a drop of life blood in their veins

With a sad smile the mother looks up at her daughter, and she remarks —

" We are better off now, dear one, than we were last night !"

"Yes, mother, yet ere the weary week is gone, our scanty store will be finished If we work night and day, we cannot earn more than two dollars, our rent here is one dollar a week Oh, it is hard for two, in the cold winter time, to live upon a dollar, yet, mother, there are others who suffer more than we!'"

"Do not speak of it, child—I would not think so But daughter, cheer me up with your voice—sing me some song, as you used to do ere we were so poor as now!'"

"I will sing for you, mother, but not one of those gay songs, which came from my heart as well as my lips in other and brighter days."

And then, in a sweet and plaintive tone, the fair girl sang

THE SEWING GIRL'S SONG

I

Wan and weary—sick and cheerless,
  By a feeble taper s light,
Sat and sang the never tearless,
  At the dreary dead of night,
          The burden of her lay
            Was work, work away,
          Thro' the night and the day,
            Was work, work away

II

We are many in the city
  Who the weary needle ply,
None to aid and few to pity
  Tho' we sicken down and die,
            But 'tis work, work away
              By night and by day,
            Oh, 'tis work, work away,
              We've no time to pray

III

Work we ever—pay is scanty,
  Scarce enough to gain us bread,
Starving in the midst of plenty,
  Better far we all were dead!
            For 'tis work, work away
              By night and by day,
            Oh, 'tis work, work away,
              We've no time to play

IV

Hearts are breaking—souls are sinking
  'Neath the heavy load they bear,
Yet live *Christians* never thinking
  What our many sorrows are,
      While we work, work away
      By night and by day,
      While we work, work away
      With scarce time to pray !

The daughter paused, for she heard the sobs of her mother—she saw the big tears gush out from her sunken eyes, like juice from the crushed grape, and her voice trembled, her own eyes filled with tears

Oh, how much more truth than poetry is there in our little song, reader

The mother looked up through her tears

"Oh ! why did you sing that sad, too truthful song, my child ? My heart was heavy before, but now its care burden is greater, for as a painting brings up a remembrance of its scenes, so do your words bring before me our lonely, miserable condition Yes, my child , better far that we were dead than thus to suffer in the very midst of a rich and beautiful city !"

"I will sing another, mother , it, too, has truth and a moral in it "

I

I'll never despair ! I'll never despair !
  My heart shall be light ,
The glance of my eye shall ever rest where
  The Hope star is bright.

II

Oh, I have seen much of trouble and strife,
  I've smiled and I've wept,
But firmly my course thro' the ocean of life
  I've still *onward* kept

III

I'm ever the same in joy or in sorrow
  In sickness or health,
Careless to day how dawneth the morrow,
  In want or in wealth

IV

I'll never despair, tho' clouds do o'ercast
   The hopes of my youth,
But fearless and bold, I'll face the rough blast
   With *honor* and *truth*

V

I'll trust to my God and the strength of his power,
   Nor bow to the blast,
As 'neath the tall oak is shelter'd the flower
   Till the storm be past

" In Him indeed is our only trust,—His creatures would care little if we did die and starve in their midst'" murmured the mother, and though her eyes were almost blinded by the tears which *would* come, she stitched away at the warm, comfortable garment which she was making

And thus with their sad but simple converse worked mother and daughter on, until the midnight hour was past, and then after bending their knees in prayer to the orphan's Father and the widow's Friend, they retired to their straw pallet and clasped in each other's arms slept,—slept from very weariness That couple had got up with the dawn of light, reader, and what think you they had earned by laboring steadily all the livelong day and evening Perhaps *twenty cents* a piece This is no fancy of mine—I have seen poor girls, pale, sickly, worn out things, working day after day, and from their own lips have learned the prices of their labor, and then, to be sure of my proof, have learned from their employers the same truths And what say these employers in excuse for thus coining their gold from the life blood of the poor?

Why, they have rivals in business—they must sell *cheap* or not at all—to sell cheap they must get their work for almost nothing, and these poor girls must work or starve, or do even worse, and they must do it at the employer's prices

Oh, many an unhappy inmate of houses of wretchedness has been driven there by this very extortion of labor, many an inmate of our city prison has been *forced* into crime and depravity, by hunger and cold, and who at the great day of judgment will be answerable for this?

Ye, who living in the lap of luxury, have no care for the suffering around ye!

It was midnight, and still this same second evening in our history, and the hell which we described before, was crowded as usual

Harry Whitmore, and his shadow, Gus Livingston, was there, and, beside them, before the long faro table stood Charles Meadows, and by the checks in his hand, as well as the excited appearance of his face, it could be seen that once more he was trying his fortune

Harry was not playing, he was only watching the play of his new friend, who, as on the night before, played a bold, reckless game, and of course a losing one At each bet his excitement grew greater, and he followed a plan which is sometimes used with success in a *fair* game—that of doubling his bet each time that he lost At last his losses became so heavy that his double would take every dollar he had with him He looked for a moment at the pile of five hundred in his hand—paused, sighed, and hesitated—perchance he thought then of his mother and sister, who, for his sake, denied themselves so many little comforts, but as he was seen thus to pause, a gentleman by his side one whom he knew to be of a good family—a man, too, in a fine business, and who could, *of course*, have no interest in the game—remarked—

" That ten spot has won twice in succession, Mr Meadows, it will be sure to run through "

" Thank you," replied the young man, and then he laid down his five hundred dollars on the ten spot, and, strange to say, it *did* win

" I'd let it lay," whispered his kind adviser, " it is sure to run through ?"

Charles Meadows did not see that by permitting his bet to win, the dealer had a haul of over a thousand from the bet of a young Englishman on another card, he thought that his luck was changing, and he let his thousand lay upon the board in order to make it two The next deal saw that thousand quietly drawn over to the banker's side, and, with a calmness caused alone by desperation, Charles Meadows smiled and said—

" Broke once more! I am, *indeed*, in luck !"

"He saw not the wink that passed between his *gentleman* adviser and the banker   He thought, of course, that all was fair   He was about to turn away, when Harry Whitmore spoke to him

"Don't give up the ship, Mr Meadows   That last bet was unlucky, but the one before was all right"

"I'm broke, sir!" was the calm answer of the young man

"Let me lend you a couple of hundred, and go you halves in your luck, be it good or bad"

"By Heaven, you are indeed a friend!   I'll take it, and give my note for it"

"Never mind the note   friends, *gentlemen*, never require such paltry papers   Your word, sir, is as good as your paper!" replied the other, at the same time handing him over the two hundred

At this moment the dealer and the banker bent slightly over towards each other, and, in a low whisper, the latter said

' We must play him a little to night   Let him win about *five*, and he ll bring a larger pile to morrow night. '

The dealer answered only with a look of assent, and the next moment the deal began   A wink had been given to the respectable *mercantile* gentleman, and though, as before, he gave his advice to Charles, the latter won upon nearly every bet

"Play with small bets, and be sure,' said he   "I wouldn't advise you to play heavy   Lay it down in fives and tens"

And the fives and tens won, of course   But as his winnings increased, the young man became more and more excited, and wished to bet heavier   At last, his pile reached the five hundred   He determined to bet all upon a single card   And now, with a smile of kindness, even Mr H , the banker, advised him not to be so rash

"You have lost too much already, Mr Meadows   Don't bet so rashly , we don t want to win your money," said he, in his usual quiet and bland way

" But I want to win my own back   I will lay this down on the Jack !" replied the young man

"No, not on the Jack, or you would be sure to lose," said Pat " Just wait until the deal is turned without putting down your money, and if that card wins, I'll make you a present of the amount !"

Meadows held back as he was requested and, sure enough, the Jack did *not* win

Pat smiled, and congratulated the young man, while the *respectable* adviser remarked, in a tone which could only be heard by the betters

"What a noble fellow Pat Hisen is ! He is the only fair gambler in town He seems to play for amusement, rather than for gain He is a thorough-bred gentleman !" And then as he turned to Meadows, he remarked

"I would advise you not to play any more to night You see your luck has changed "

"What do *you* say, Mr Whitmore ? I feel as if I was playing for you now," said Charles, addressing himself to his new friend.

"Well, as you have already more than doubled my loan, I think we might as well drop down to Bardotte s or Florence's, and eat a few invigorators, of the " York Bay' or " Saddle Rock" brand, and then go on a *bender*, kick up a row in Leonard street, or bother the ' Charlies' a little "

" Be it as you will Here s your money back, and the half of the winnings " cried young Meadows

" Never mind that, Charley, my boy We'll need it to night, you shall be the purser Keep it to pay our way with," replied young Whitmore, carelessly

And the next moment Gus Livingston took a chance to whisper into the ear of Meadows—

" A capital fellow is Harry ! Rich as Crœsus, and free as water !"

Reader while these young men are wending their way to the oyster saloon, we will tell you what the two *inseparables* are

Harry Whitmore is a descendant of one of the first families has had the advantages of education and travel, and is what the world calls a finished gentleman He rides, dances, shoots, and fences well, speaks several of the modern languages, is skilled in music, and has a very ready flow of conversation He is withal a " ladies' man ,"—but more, he is a consummate, heartless libertine He is not rich, for the patrimony which he inherited from a kind grandfather is now run through, and his only funds come from a fond and too indulgent mother, whose property is so secured, that, during her lifetime, he can have no hold upon it

His father died years ago   He gambles—generally with success, because he links in with the gamblers and helps them   His fine person, plausible manners, and the " report " which he ever keeps up of being still very wealthy, enables him to be a very efficient aid to the " gentlemen with dark continuations "

Gustave Livingston, his ever present shadow, is one of that genus which is so necessary to a character like Whitmore—a kind of echo—ever ready to drink with him, or fight for him—an ever present umpire ready to turn the scale of dispute in his friend's favor, ready alike to aid him in cheating or in cajoling a victim

He, too, is a descendant of a good family   But, alas! for " fallen aristocracy," he has not only lost their wealth, but their virtues, and he is now emphatically nothing more or less than a genteel *sponge*   There are a goodly number of his class in Gotham

CHAPTER IV

THERE is a house in Cherry street, not far from Catherine Market —a low, frame house, painted yellow—a two storied, dormant windowed building, which is well known to every police officer in the city, and their visits to it have been frequent

A little to the north of its door stands an old time tree, and for many a year it has been known to the "crossmen" and "knucks" of the town as "Jack Circle's watering place" and "fence " The dirty red curtains before the windows signify that grog is to be had within, and seldom did it happen, either by day or night, that Harriet, the daughter of Jack, who acted as bar maid, did not have plenty of occupation in attending to the guests   The house, as I said, is a low, mean looking frame, but, as it runs back, is much larger than it appears

Jack Circle seldom attended the bar himself, but either moved about among his customers, conversing with them, or absented himself in the back room, where none save himself and a chosen few could enter, for this was a kind of general assembling room for the English burglars and pickpockets, who, driven from their own land, pursued their "profession" in New York   They had another hall, which we soon will describe, but this was a kind of meeting, smoking, and drinking room   And Jack Circle was their chief—they having formed themselves into a regular confederacy, agreeing to act only upon the orders of their chief, which were to be given after a consultation with the gang in assembly And the gang had their regular weekly meetings, when the report of each member was as duly given to the chief, as the reports of the city police are to their worthy head

On the same evening which dates with the events of our last chapter, there was a very "select party" in the little dark back room in the second story of old Jack's house, to whom we will introduce you, reader

3

First, let Mr Jack Circle stand before you   He is large, very portly, red faced, jolly, Toby Philpot kind of a looking fellow, and yet a man of immense muscular power   The bull doggish look about his eyes and mouth—the thick, short neck—the broad, round shoulders and full chest, proclaim him to be what he is,—an Englishman of the real St Giles's order   His age is fifty or a little more, but like the general run of men of his class, that age leaves him just in his prime   He is, and long has been, the chief of the gang to whom we devote this chapter

His daughter, Harriet, is well known as Tom Walker's wife, to all the crossmen of the town, of whom she has ever been a favo rite, judging from the fact that she has now some four or five husbands, for as soon as one of them got jugged and found a tem porary home in the State prison, she would get another, until she is so well supplied, that she generally has one on hand all the time   She was, at the dating of our story, about twenty five years of age, not ill looking, though in no way remarkable for extreme beauty   She was, however, tall, well formed, and very powerful, and possessed a great influence over the cracksmen of her clan

And now for one more of the party—Mr Bob Sutton   You have, of course, heard of him, reader   He is a perfect hero among burglars, his name has been connected with every daring bur glary that has occurred here within twenty years   He is nearly as old as Jack Circle, has a rather open and honest looking face when not on the cross, is very large and stout   In some rough bout or other, he has had his cut water staved in—in other words, his nose has been broken in till it is rather flat   Scars are seen like a map of pugilistic history all over his broad coun tenance   He was once quite a celebrated pugilist in England He is known generally as " Bob the Wheeler," because he was in his younger days brought up to the trade of a wheelwright   He was once sentenced to Sing Sing for life, but was pardoned out, and is now a greater rascal than ever

Then comes Bill Hoppy   He too has been gazetted so often in our city papers, that his name is as well known as John Smith's He is rather a good looking fellow of thirty years of age, with dark eyes, black curling hair, is 5 feet 9 inches high, ever gen teelly apparelled, and is as daring a cove as ever cracked a crib, touched a dummy, or palmed a glisten

Jack Shaw—a tall, burly looking, but well formed customer, with a slight cast in his left eye, which makes him "look two ways for a Sunday"—is another of our friends   And with "Black Bill," alias Jack Henderson, makes up the party who, on the evening in question, were assembled in the little up stairs room   "Black Bill" gets his sobriquet from his black muzzled, dark and forbidding appearance   He is tall, rough-looking, resembling somewhat an old second mate, who, broken for some misdemeanor aboard ship, becomes the worst fore mast hand that ever grumbled at an order, or kicked up a mutiny   He is thirty five or seven, and to use the words of one who *knows* him, "looks the thief all over" Nearly all of these fellows are "*caffers*"—a slang term applied to the convicts of Botany Bay   In a future place the term, and its origin, will be explained   Mr   Jack Circle has a peculiar right to the title

The whole of them are English, their language is flash, and they can boast of relatives in Botany Bay, and of others who have reached quite as elevated positions as Mahomet's coffin

But to their meeting

" Ve are all here, my covies," said old Jack, when he glanced around the room, which was lighted by the one side of a regular thief's lantern , " let's hear wot's on the lay ! Wot 'ave you got to say Bobby, my lucky ?"

" Vy, Cap'n Jack, there's a crib as I've got my peepers on where they will stir their tea with silver spoons, ven we knows that pewter is better for their 'ealths "

" Can it be cracked heasy ? '

" Bout as heasy as gettin' into an old shoe "

" Vel, then, crack it, my lucky , but do it up right ! Vot 'ave you got to say, Bill ?"

" I knows of a Gospel shop w'ere they takes in their Sunday dimes on silver plates, and sarves up their goodies on the same sort o' stuff   Ve might as vel eat off o' silver onst, jist to see 'ow the vittels 'ud taste !"

" Right as a trivet, my cove, you is a prig of the old sort ! Vot 'ave you got to say, Jack ?"

" Nothin' more than that !" and Shaw threw down a bag which seemed by its sound to contain silver, and a goodly amount

" Them ere's the werry answers as I like best !'" cried Harriet " 'Ow much 'ave you lifted, Jack ?"

" A matter of five hundred, or so   I prigged two prancers and sold 'em , 'elped a swell to carry his gold thimble , borried two cloaks for my uncle from ' the Astor,' and picked up a dummy for a green 'un, and went 'im 'alves !"

" Oh Jack, times is a gettin' low," sighed Black Bill

" Vy , 'ow so ?   I dosent see but as I've done sumthin' tow'rd payin' the scot this week "

" But it's been in sich a small way," replied Bill, with another sigh   " The time wos when we would'nt touch at nothin' less than cracking a big crib , and now it's enough to break my heart to see a man of your talent and standing forced to prig prancers, knuck tickers, and go on the low sneaks !   I'm agoing to quit the profession !"

"Quit !" exclaimed all, in surprise   "Quit the profession, Bill?"

" Yes , I'm agoin' into a respectable business !"

" Vot is it, Bill—vont you take me in for an active partner ?" added Harriet

" Vot *do* you mean to do, Bill ?" said old Jack

" Why, cap'n, I mean to open a jewelry store !"

" Open a jewelry store, you noddy !" cried Harriet, " 'ow're you goin' to do that, 'ven you hav'nt got no more stock than a broken down sheney ?"

" Why, my duck, I'm agoin' to open it with a jimmy and a dark lantern, to be sure !"

"Ha ! ha !" shouted the old man , " allers at your jokin', my lucky   You're the cove as never died a cryin' !   'Ave you found a bang up lay ?"

" I haint found nothin' else !"

" Vere away is it ?"

" In Boston, the coppers there aint half so keen with their peepers as they are here !   I went on and borried the 'amount o' my expenses from a swell that put up at the Tremont !   I did it against my will, for I'm above little actions, and I've got no small wices, but I was short of the dust, and had to do it to pay expenses "

" 'Ow many of the boys vill it take to crack the jewel shop ? '

" Why, I want Jack and Bill Hoppy, and then I want a young

ster for a snakesman, one as can get in through a hole in the back winder " '

" When do you want to go on the dub ?"

" The sooner the better, as the gal said when her man asked her the day "

The chief paused a moment, and seemed to be counting up the other engagements in his mind, when three, low, double taps, were heard at the door

" Its von uv us, Arriet, my gal," said old Jack, and the woman at once unbarred the door

The person who entered, was " Charley Cooper," the same dapper little fellow, who in our first chapter addressed Big Lize in Broadway

" Ello, Charley, my kid ! tip us your mawley, vot is'nt new to-night ?" cried old Jack, reaching out his mawley or hand to the new comer

" Nothin' much worth pattering about Lize made a big haul last night, I've brought it over to put in the big bag, and draw our share of the lucky "

" 'Ow did she make the raise ?"

" Got a big bug home with her, and jist then her usband came up stairs, and the swell did'nt have no time to count his change afore he got out "

" Come the panel over him, eh ? Was the swell a gold finch ?"

" He was'nt nothin' else Got a clear ten times ten out of him "

" Won't he pay a wisit to old Hays ?" asked Harriet

" I reckon not, he had grey hairs on his head, and maybe he would'nt like to have it known where his breeches were when the dummy was touched "

" Vel, my kiddies, ve might as vel count up the veek's earnins, and divide the lucky," cried old Jack, " I'll keep ' Cupid's ' share, and 'Tilda's and the rest for 'em till they come, you're all a losin' time, as the devil said to the parson ven his congergashun vas asleep "

And then old Jack bade Harriet trim the glim, and all the spoils for the week were laid out, and the division made

After this was done, quite an animated discussion occurred, as to what the gang should next do   Henderson was opposed to all small work, and was bent on opening his jewelry store, to which Hoppy assented only on the condition of their helping him first to sack the " gospel shop "   Each of the party had some new place upon which his eye had fallen during the week, and the dangers of detection and the prospect of success in each case, was duly discussed , old Jack, from his long experience and extensive knowledge, having the loudest say in the party

At last all was settled, a visiting party of inspection appo nted for the Boston lay, and then the party adjourned to the less secret room below, for the purpose of taking a bout at drinking and smoking   Harriet of course was their attendant, while old Jack being through *official* business once again mingled with his out side customers, many of whom were petty thieves, &c , who, though not connected with his gang in any way, used his house as a fencing ken, or place of deposit for their stealings   No one would give a better price than Jack for a set of spoons   No one could smash a fifty or a check better, and as none save thieves visited his house, they were pretty safe there

Another picture, reader   A young man is seen sitting in a large arm chair, one of that leather backed easy kind, so fashion able in the better sort of lawyer's offices , before him is a centre table heaped up with books of all kinds, and printed in nearly all languages   With his heels cocked up on the edge of the table and a fine cigar between his lips, the young man seemed intently engaged in reading a small octavo work, and while he read, ever and anon an approving smile or appreciating remark could be seen and heard, as his eye met pleasing passages

The room looked like a perfect literary museum, though its contents did not seem to be very classically arranged, for there were large heaps piled upon the floor in every corner, covered with dust , some of them neat, elegantly bound works, others without covers, ancient looking volumes   Maps, pictures, ink stands, writing materials, were scattered all around in rare confu sion, intermixed with clothes, domestic utensils, &c , &c   But by far the greatest amount of the contents of the room was in books

The young man seemed to be eighteen or twenty years of age, was a fine, interesting, scholarlike looking individual, dressed in a plain suit of black, wearing a white neckcloth, and having a ra ther the appearance of a student of divinity   A wide, Byronical collar was thrown back to display a very white and well turned neck , his curling black hair was carelessly brushed back from a high, ample brow , and if we are to judge from the usual description of them, he looked very like a young *poet*

Reader, this young man, *Frank Hennock,* is now in Sing Sing, serving out his term of punishment for a grand larceny   You will in our romance learn more of him

He was, as we have said above, seated in his easy chair, in a room filled with the proceeds of his plunder, and he was engaged in reading very attentively the first volume of Bulwer's Paul Clifford   He paused, raised his eyes up from the book and took his feet down from the table, as three low taps were heard at his door, then he still waited until three double taps followed, when he said

"'Tis one of us, it's O K," and proceeded to unbolt the door

A rather good looking female, of twenty three or five years apparent age, crossed the threshold, to whom he extended his hand, exclaiming

" Ah, is it thee, my fair Matilda?   My heart like the wilting flower has longed for the sunlight of thy smiles, and thy presence is as pleasant as it was unlooked for "

" Oh, blast your humbuggery—talk plain English to me—I'm not used to it   Patter flash, my lucky, you're as used to it as I am "

" Flash, Matilda ! oh horrible, it is vulgar   Byron, Tom Moore, Walter Scott, all favorite authors of mine, never used it Why, here is Bulwer   I'm reading his Paul Clifford, and he don t use flash language in a dozen places   In all my collection I've got but one book on the flash, and that's Captain Grose's dictionary   No, it's vulgar, and I won't use it, Matilda "

" Vulgar or not, it's mighty useful at times "

" Yes, and I'll use it when it is necessary, but Matilda, when I am in thy sweet presence I would prefer to address thee in language more refined "

" Oh——sugar, you know what I'm used to, what the deuce do you want to make out as if I was an angel for ?"

" Ah, Matilda, to me you are an angel, a guardian angel, I

may say   When I was jugged the last time did'nt you play the affectionate sister for me, and bring me all I wanted ?"

" Well, I did'nt do no more than I ought to, Frank, you'd do as much for me, would'nt you ?'"

" Yes, peerless one, I'd deliberately lay me down and expire for you!   Matilda, I love you !'"

" Prove it !'"

" How shall I ? must I scale the frozen cliffs of snow capped Orizabo ?   Must I fly to the burning shores of ebon Africa, and bring thence the hide of the Nehemian lion ?   Must I throw Van Amburg in the shade, and enter boldly in between the jaws of Welch's elephant ?   Speak, fair possessor of my heart, speak and I will thy will obey !'"

" Oh, blast the thing, Frank, speak like a man of sense ! You're as good a knuck as ever frisked a swell !   Why don't you make a *raise* ?'"

" Why, to tell the truth, my love, I'm so much taken up with my literary pursuits, that, on my honor, I've no time to devote to the less elegant, but I acknowledge the more profitable avocation to which you allude   And besides, 'Tilda, I have another objec tion !'"

" What's that ?'"

" Why, to tell the truth, my fair friend, I've not got the spunk to make a real large haul   When I hear of the boys making a large lift, I always envy them, but somehow or other whenever I think of trying at something large, my heart fails me !'"

" You're a spooney, I'll tell you what it is, with sich a father and brother as you have, you ought to be ashamed of yourself for doing so little, youv'e never done a nothin for the honor of your family, when your precious daddy and your brother has both ' lifted ' themselves into notoriety "

" Ah, Matilda, now don't speak of them, they are unfortunate individuals   I can see them now within the dreary walls of Sing Sing, yes, I was thinking of them this very morning, for I com posed a poem on the subject   I'll read it to you—"

" No, no !'" cried the woman, interrupting him, " I've other fish to fry   We've got business for you !'"

" For me, what is it, my love ?"

" Why there's a swell up town as has advertised for a private secretary, some kind of a clark, you know, and old Jack has found out from Sheney Bill, the Intelligence office keeper, all about the old cove He's rich as thunder and close as a wolf trap !"

" Well, what have I to do with that ?"

" Why, you've got to git the sitervation ! The recommend ations are all made out, you're to be the only son of your poor widdered mother, you know, to have 'sperienced religion, and all that   The old cove goes in for all that kind of humbug "

" Well, what is to come after that ?"

" Why, you poor noddy, can't you see ! Get everything right, find out where he stows his precious, get the run of the house, and old Jack 'll send some of the boys to help you take care of him and his money !"

" Oh, 'Tilda, if I do this, I shall be guilty of ing atitude, that monstrous crime which Shakspeare calls—"

" Oh, curse your Shakspeare, and you too   Why don't you attend to your business   Jack has sent for you and you've got to go   Here's the *pape's*"—and the girl handed him the letters of recommendation—" the where he lives is on the back of them, so cut for your lay, or old Jack 'll be down on you with somethin as 'll get you in the jug afore you knows where you is !"

" Well, 'Tilda, if I must, I must   I hope the old covey has got a good librafy   Ah, 'Tilda, you don't know what you lose by not being acquainted with literary pursuits "   And the young man breathed a commiserating sigh

" I don't know nothin' about no persuits, 'cept the nab's per suits, and I'll be blasted if I likes them overly and above com mon ," replied the girl, and then she turned and left the room

For a moment Frank looked after her, then striking an atitude, cried —

" Thou art gone—thou art gone, like the last rose of summer, and left me alone !"   Then glancing at the papers which he held in his hand, he changed his voice and attitude into a very good imitation of Charles Kean, and cried —

" To go or not to go ? that is the question ! Whether it will be better for me to stop here and read novels or to go and make a raise worthy of the glorious profession followed by Paul Clifford and other heroic men !"

Again he paused, and then striking an attitude imitative of Anderson, continued

"Yes, I will go I see a vision before me ! Be thou a spirit of wealth or a goblet damned, bringst with thee airs from Sing Sing, or thoughts of Blackwell's, I go Be the intent wicked— its shape questionable, I care not ! I cry—go on ! I will follow thee—yes, death or glory is my motto—Paul Clifford like, I'll *do* or *die* !'"

He seemed to have adopted the latter thought, for, after slicking down his hair and arranging his neat, but thread bare suit of black, before one of his many looking glasses, he departed on his errand, carefully locking the door behind him

CHAPTER V

At the close of our fourth chapter, we left three individuals in the street, who were bent upon having, what our fashionable bucks call " *a real bender*," and now, reader, with or without your consent we will " see them through "

First, Charles Meadows, Harry Whitmore, and Gustave Li vingston, bent their way to Florence's for a few of the salt water vegetables, or invigorators, as Harry facetiously termed them

" Two stews and a raw," were soon stowed away in their victu alling holds, and then fortifying the inner man with a little of the " B B B ," the party felt prepared for the evening, or rather for the morning, as the old City hall bell had told *one* sometime pre vious to the moment which found them standing upon the *pavé* at the corner of Park Place

The streets were now nearly deserted , the night nymphs had slunk away to their dens , only here and there the ever vigilant " stars " could be seen on their beats, examining each hole and corner with searching glances, lest some thief or loafer should have made a berth which belonged not unto him Now and then a person would hurry swiftly by, but he was perchance speeding to the doctor's office to procure aid for some one suffering in the agony of illness , and then again one would be seen close muf fling his face in his cloak, stealing cautiously along, as if he had been guilty of something of which he was ashamed Perhaps he was slinking home to the arms of an affectionate and waiting wife, and he too coming from the gambling house, or a place of even greater infamy for him

The young men came up from the fashionable saloon, and as they paused upon the pave, Harry cried

" Well, fellows, where shall we go ? I say, Charley, (excuse the familiarity, but by Jove, I love you like a brother), which way shall we start ?"

" I don't care a copper, old boy, it's late now, my mother and sister have gone to bed, and I'll make a night of it," replied the young man

" Have you got a sister? How old is she?" asked Harry quickly

" Only sixteen, and she's the prettiest girl in York, if I do say it"

" Prettier than mine, do you think? They say *my* sister is *some* in a crowd"

" Well, you shall see for yourself, Harry—by Jove, you shall I'll bet the drinks on her beauty and leave it to yourself after you've seen her "

" No, I'll take the bet, but you shall see my sister, and then I'll leave it to you to decide," cried Harry, and had Charles Meadows looked him in the face at the moment by the lamp light, he might have seen the sly wink which was given to Gus Living ston, to keep up the rig, for Gus knew well that Harry Whitmore was an only child

Like a good echo or sponge assistant as he was, he added to his friend's last remark

" If your sister is'nt an angel, Charley, you'll lose the bet Maria Whitmore is'nt a girl that can be matched in every crowd "

" Well—we'll see," replied young Meadows, " but it's getting late now, and we'd better be on the move "

" It's getting *early*, you mean, but it is just the fashionable hour for the Leonard street ladies, they're in full blast there about this hour "

" When do the poor creatures sleep?" asked Charles

" Why, in the day, to be sure, how *green* you are," replied Harry   " You don't seem to know much about the fashions "

" I have never mingled with that class, yet," replied the young man—" until I got into the infernal habit of gambling, I always spent my evenings at home with my mother and Isabella "

" Isabella! Is that your sister's name?"

" Yes—and my mother's also "

" 'Tis a sweet one   I have always liked that name "

" And I, because my pure, angelic sister, owns it "

The eye of Whitmore flashed with pleasure   In a low whisper he said to his echo

" Gus, this must be something great, eh? Sixteen, pure, *green*, he means I must see the bird "

The *echo* only answered with a smile and glance of more than *wordy* meaning

" Well, where shall it be? At Julia B 's, 55 Leonard, or some other of hell's paradises," cried Harry

" Where you please," replied Charles, " as I said before, I am not acquainted with these localities or their mysteries "

" Then 'tis high t me you were initiated, we're the chaps that *can* show you round! eh, Gus?"

" To be sure we are Why, Harry knows every pretty girl that s out," replied the echo in answer to this appeal

" Then to Jule's let it be," cried Harry, and the young men wrapped their cloaks around them and staggered up the now al most deserted street They soon reached Leonard street, down this they turned toward the North River But a little way down and they paused before a large, fine looking brick house, up the steps of which they passed and rang the bell In a moment a little shutter at one side of the door was raised, and a female voice asked

" Who is there?"

" It s me, Mary I'm here with two friends of the right sort " replied Harry

" Who s *me*?" answered the facetious door keeper, " I don't know anybody of that name "

" Well, you know Harry Whitmore, don't you?"

" Oh, yes, Harry, is that you?" cried the woman

"To be sure it is, and it's as cold as Norway out here, stir your stumps and let us in, that's a good Molly "

In a moment the heavy bolts were drawn back, the green paint ed iron door swung heavily on its hinges, and the young men were within the most celebrated *palace* of infamy which disgraces Gotham

As the door closed behind them, they could hear joyous voices within, gay peals of laughter, and the sound of the piano also fell upon their ears The next instant they were in the large double parlor, where were already quite a number of " *gentle-men*," some of them grey haired men, but all having the appear ance of being *monied* individuals, for here, as well as in the gam bler's hell, no one is wanted, who is not the possessor of all powerful gold

There were a dozen or eighteen females, seated on the splendid ottomans around the room, all of them good looking, some of them very handsome They were dressed very richly, though in a manner calculated to exhibit the beauty of their forms, even at the expense of modesty Low necked dresses revealed even more than bare, powdered shoulders, their arms were unsleeved, and those who had pretty feet, wore skirts sufficiently short to exhibit them They were curled, and powdered and painted, until art could do no more to add to their looks, and now the poor miserable creatures were on exhibition, as pieces of finery ready for sale

And they seemed gay, appeared to be happy They laughed and danced and sang as if their path was strewn with flowers, yet, as beneath a glistening like in the calm summer time, a wreck may be hidden, so beneath that outward gaiety many a broken heart lay cold and still, many a wrecked spirit and crushed hope was concealed They then, amid the glare of lights, the reflection of the crimson velvet curtains and the gorgeous furniture, looked as if they possessed beauty, but could they have been seen without their paint and ornaments, without the artificial aids around them, pale would then be their now rosy cheeks, sunken their lustreless eyes, gone the smile, and hushed the laugh

And many of these poor hapless creatures were young—fifteen, sixteen, seventeen years of age—too young, oh Heaven ! for tha living grave And how came they there ? Let the lawless, heartless, God forsaken libertines answer, who led some of them away by false promises from the paths of honor—let them reply ! Woman—fond, trusting, all confiding woman, but too often listens to their honeyed words But there are yet other causes which lead them there Many a poor girl, possessing nothing save beauty, has toiled and suffered for many a weary winter's day, and for her toil, like our poor sewing girl, has not been able to sustain even the semblance of comfort, or keep her chilled limbs warm While thus suffering, she has seen the courtesan pass along, robed in silks and furs—at least *dressed* warmly, even richly And while the thought of her daily toil and her own misery was contrasted with the lot of the other, she has yielded to the voice of the tempter, and fallen into the pit whence no hand amid all our *Christian* city will attempt to raise her If she had been able to live by her honorable labor, that poor girl would rather have died than have sprung into the dead sea of pollution and infamy

Reader, excuse us, but this is a book where we must at times break aside from the thread of our story to moralize He were worse than thoughtless, who could see and describe the scenes which we have, and not give some reflections thereupon

When our *trio* entered the splendid parlor, they were met by the beautiful hostess in person

"Good evening Harry, I'm glad to see you and Gus You have a friend, I perceive," said she in a bland and musical tone

"Yes, Jule," replied Harry, "my very particular friend, Mr Meadows He is rather verdant, but you'll find him a glorious fellow, quite 'one of us,' I assure you"

"I doubt it not, nature has kindly written his character upon his face" And the "*lady*" reached out a very white and richly jeweled hand, while she smiled most sweetly Then she added

"I will introduce you to some of my boarders, sir You will find quite a variety We have blondes and brunettes The creole of the South, the lily of the central States, and the snow drop of the North Take my arm and walk around with me"

The young man hesitated a moment, he saw several merchants there—men who knew him—and the fear for an instant flashed across his mind, that his employer would hear of this visit But then he thought that, of course, for their own sakes, the *respectable* individuals would keep the secret, and he accepted the arm of Mrs B, while Harry and Gus seated themselves on a sofa between a couple of girls who were already half tipsy on champagne, and, to use their own language, "were as full of fun as an egg could be of meat"

"What is the style of beauty which you most admire?" asked the lady patroness

"Why, really, I know not I admire all kinds, I believe" replied Charles "It would be hard to say, but"—and the young man glanced at his companion as he spoke—"I think dark, languishing eyes, dark hair, a form full, even a little *embon*

point , and a complexion at once clear and fair may be consi
dered beautiful "   •

Both her lip and eye smiled, as his companion saw the drift of
his compliment , but without appearing to notice it, she said

" Then I must introduce you to a young lady from Baltimore ,
or really from a city a little beyond."

Then as they paused before a very pretty and lady like looking
girl, the hostess added

" Mr. Meadows, Miss Kate Hall   You will find Miss Kate a
very agreeable companion, sir , but she seems dull to night, I
think a bottle of champagne will be of service to you both "

" Order it, of course," replied Meadows   And then the in
teresting young lady moved aside and left room for him to sit
upon the ottoman which she occupied   As he did this, he remarked

" You do seem sad this evening Miss , may I ask the reason ?"

The young lady sighed, looked down upon the beautiful fan
which she flirted in her hand, and in a low, sweet tone, replied

" Really, sir—we are strangers, and beside, I am not very
sad "   But as if to give the lie to her own words, her bosom
heaved with even a deeper sigh than before

Meadows felt interested   The girl really was very pretty
She seemed exceedingly lady like   And while he took her hand
in his with a gentle pressure, he continued

" Do tell me, Miss Kate   I can sympathise with you , and if
I can aid you, heaven knows that I will !' "

The lady gently returned the pressure of his hand   She looked
up at him , he thought that a tear was gathering in her bright
eyes , but she dropped them again beneath the shadow of her
long lashes, and another sigh came from her lips   She made no
other reply , and this made Charles only the more pressing to
know what was the cause of her sorrow

At this moment the champagne was brought before them, the
cork flew from the long necked bottle, and Charles receiving the
two brimming glasses from the waiter, handed one to his com
panion, who simply placed it to her lips, then, without drinking,
set the glass again upon the salver

" Will you not take your wine ?" asked Meadows , and there
was tender solicitation in his tone

"I thank you," replied the girl, "but I seldom touch wine It is not that which can raise *my* spirits," and once more she sighed

Oh do tell me—do tell me, Miss Kate, what your sorrows are I feel for you—will alleviate them if it be in my power I will be as a brother to you!"

"A *brother!*" murmured she, and now she hid her face in her handkerchief, while she continued—"I had a brother once, one who, if he had lived, never would have seen me here in this dreadful place, leading a life so full of brimming misery! Oh, sir, if you knew all, you would pity me!" and now he could hear her sob

"I do pity you, dear girl, indeed I do Tell me all, I must hear it, I will aid you '

"There are too many listeners here the others would jeer and laugh at me if they heard all that I would say "

"Then why not go to another room, have not you a room ?"

"But sir, you have been so kind—your voice is so full of pure sympathy for me, I cannot ask you up there, where, Heaven knows, I have spent hours of misery! My room is up stairs,' and then she falte ed, sighed again, and in a tremulous tone added—"there is a bed in it !"

"It matters not, you need not fear me, I only wish to hear of your sorrows—to alleviate them if I can," cried the young man And now he set down his untasted glass of wine

' I cannot deny any request from one so kind and noble as yourself," said the girl, and she arose to lead the way After they had reached the hall, as they were about to ascend the stair case which led into the second story, Miss Kate made an excuse to return to the room for her handkerchief, which she had " *acci dentally*" dropped, but had Charles returned with her, he would have seen her pause by the side of Mrs B, to whom she whis pered

"I've caught him, Julia ! I came the *sentimental* over him, and I think I'll make a *few* out of him! He is going up stairs to listen to a tale of sorrow "

The hostess smiled sweetly, and as Kate walked away, re marked to a gambler looking man who sat by her side

"Kate is the most profitable girl in my house Jack "

4

Reader, we will not linger here in this garden of corruption. We could, if we would, show you such mysteries and miseries here as you little dream of, but this is a book in which we have pledged ourself not to write one line that we would not lay before a young sister's eye. It would be impossible for us to dwell upon the scenes here and describe them as they are, without overstepping that pledge. Therefore, we will leave Harry and Gus drinking champagne with their already drunken companions, and Charles Meadows to listen to a hackneyed story, which will only end in his giving Miss Kate all the money in his pocket to save her from the impending misfortune, which has made her so sad, and we will leave her so overcome with his nobleness and generosity, that she cannot part with him that evening, and let you imagine more or less as you choose.

CHAPTER VI

In one of those beautiful streets which stretch across from Broadway to the North River, not far from Union Square, stands among many, a two story brick building with a small yard in front, which is protected by an iron railing The building is very neat , its brass knobs on the door and bell wire are brightly polish ed, there is not a speck of dirt upon the marble door steps Even the little evergreen trees in the yard are trimmed down with quaker like neatness The window blinds are closed and the house seems still and quiet, as if it was not inhabited

The time when all this so appeared, was but a day or two after the first date in our story

If that house looked cold and rather cheerless without, it was far from being so within In the back parlor, which was quite richly furnished, sat a rather corpulent gentleman, who seemed rather past the prime of his life, of fifty or fifty five years appa rently He sat upon a sofa, which was drawn up in front of a glowing coal fire, and was engaged in reading one of our city periodicals There was a spice of dandyism in his dress and manner—an eye glass hung dangling from his neck, which, of course, was worn more for ornament than use, since he seemed to read easily without raising it to his eye Everything in the room wore the same appearance of neatness which we have observed before in the outside appearance of the dwelling Each book upon the centre table was laid at an equal distance from its next neighbor—each article of furniture was free from dust, and placed in exact positions about the room

The gentleman who sat alone here, was also, in his dress and looks, as neat as the room His hair, which once had been black and in fact was now only sprinkled lightly with grey, was brushed up into a peak which concealed a baldness of the crown, and it was also combed down at the side to meet a pair of rather heavy but well curled half whiskers, which, by their jetty blackness, showed that they had been dyed

Reader, this is Mr Peter Precise, who has just retired from the business of soap and candle making, in which he has realised quite a fortune, and, moreover, he has but recently learned that he possesses an interest in a family property in England or is supposed to, for, on the mother's side, he is a descendant of the cele brated " *Hunt* family" of England   His character and his name are very like   During his business life, he never varied in anything, never lost a debt, or failed to pay one, for, in the first place, he would credit no one without a precise knowledge of the means of paying, in the second, he never bought anything that he could not pay for

He was a bachelor, not because he did not like the female sex, but because he could never find a woman who did everything by rule as he did,—who rose at just such a minute each day, retired at just such an hour each night, and did just so much work   He never kept a hand in his employment, who did more or less than he was required—a single blot upon his ledger would be the surety for his book keeper's dismissal, even if his wagon horse stumbled, Mr P would sell him and get another   In early life he always said that he would retire from business when he had acquired a fortune of fifty thousand dollars, and as his books were balanced at the end of each month, he knew at that time the precise amount of his p operty   And on the very day when he found that he really was the owner of the $50,000, he gave up his concern to one who had long been his clerk, paid eight thousand dollars for the house and lot which we have described, and retired to pass the rest of his life in comfort

But he found that he was exceedingly lonesome, now that he had given up business, his very regularity had become so habitual that each morning found him up at his old hour, and frequently before he remembered that he had retired, he would be on his way to the " old stand "   He had quite a good library, and with it possessed some taste for reading   To this, and a correspondence with several lawyers and members of the Hunt family, he had now devoted himself, and in consequence of the labor of letter writing and his loneliness also, he had advertised for " an intelligent, neat, discreet young man, to act as a clerk and companion to an elderly gentleman, retired from active business "

One of the many Intelligence office keepers, a man known to Jack Circle and his gang, as Sheney Bill (the word Sheney, among them, means Jew) had seen this advertisement, and at once, in connection with Jack, had taken means to supply the said " intelligent and discreet young man," as we have seen in our last interview with Mr Frank Hennock

As we said before, Mr Precise was seated upon his sofa, which was drawn before the fire, reading, when he heard his door bell ring   He did not lay down his periodical, but he ceased to read, and listened, while the servant, who came up from the basement kitchen, answered the ring

In a moment she came to the parlor door, and announced that a young man, a very nice looking young man, was at the door, who wished to see Mr P Precise

" Tell him to come in, Jenny, my dear '" said Mr P in a quiet tone, " and see that he wipes his feet on the door mat, Jenny "

The girl turned away to obey, and Mr Precise getting his eye glass to his left eye, in the most fashionable style, awaited the appearance of

MR FRANK HENNOCK

The following engraving is illustrative of that meeting

Mr Precise saw a rather pale, and very steady looking young man before him, and for a few moments gazed at him, from head

to foot, as if he would read his character in the glance Frank seemed to feel that much depended on that look, for simply bowing, without speaking, he remained in a respectful posture, until Mr Precise took down his glass and said

" You may step forward, young man   You ha e come to apply for the situation of private secretary with me, eh ?"

" Yes, Sir   Here are letters for you," and Frank produced what Matilda Horton had called " the papes "

Mr P took them and glanced over the contents of each   Then again raising his eyes to Frank, he scanned him with another long and steady look

" Looks neat—rather thread bare, but neat '" he muttered in soliloquy —" hands clean , wonder if he uses my soap—hair nicely brushed—clean shirt—looks as if he would do, but musn't trust to looks "

Then addressing Frank, he asked—

" Can you write a good hand—no scratching or blotting eh ?"

" Yes, sir—I will give you a sample, off hand, if you wish '" replied Frank, in a very meek tone

" You shall   Go to that secretary, upon which stands the book case, let down the draw leaf, of which here is the key   In the right hand drawer find paper , in the pigeon hole above it is pens , ink is at the right hand corner   Take them and draw me up a letter "

" What kind of a letter, sir ?"

" Such a one as you would have written, if I had addressed you and offered you the situation that you ask for '"

Frank did as he was directed, and in the course of a couple of minutes, handed the letter to Mr P

The latter read it, muttering as he did so " Very neat—well worded—no blots—letters well formed   You ve been to school—studied hard—good boy, eh ?"

" I have studied and read much, sir '"

" Fond of reading, eh ?   You shall read to me—'twill be a good way of passing the long winter evenings   What do you like to read best ?"

" I prefer religious works, sir, but sometimes read poetry '

" Read to me "

" I will read you a poem of my own, sir, if you please "

' What! young man, can you write poetry yourself? You're an extraordinary lad!"

" I have written a little verse at times, sir, yet, I dare not call it poetry," replied Frank, very modestly

" Well, sir, I'll judge of that for myself If you have your poem about you, read it "

Frank drew a much worn piece of paper from his pocket, and was about to commence reading, when Mr P interrupted him, by bidding him draw a chair and sit down

This order obeyed, Frank again raised the paper, but before reading, said

" I must tell you, sir, how I came to write upon the subject I offer to you I had been out all day in search of a situation, and was going home to my mother, when I thought of going through one of the poorer parts of the city, and oh! sir, you cannot believe how much misery I saw in that walk I did so wish that I was rich, to help the poor creatures, for I saw them ragged! yes, almost naked, some of them in the street and they looked so hun gry !"

" You are a good boy, I believe!" said Mr P, evidently moved by this mark of Frank's feeling, and then ne added " You wrote this poem about them, did you?"

" Yes, sir, I will read it to you now I call it

" PITY THE POOR

I

" The winter times are coming fast,
Pipes loud and shrill the autumn blast,
And leafless limbs are quivering,
And houseless ones are shivering,
  With your eye
  You may spy
  Naked feet
  'Mid the sleet,
Then pity oh! pity the poor,
Who stand in the cold at your door!

II

" When your hearth fire blazeth brightly,
Even as it burneth nightly,

When you hear the wild winds, chilly
Pipe their warnings loud and shrilly
  In the storm
  See the form
  Thin and pale,
  Hear the wail
Of the suffering , list the cry,
' Help the poor ! Help them, or they die !'

III

" Clothed in rags so thin and scanty,
 Live they in some cheerless shanty ,
 Doors unhung and windows open,
 Roof all leaky walls all broken ,
  There half dead
  Without bread
  Hear them cry
  ' Must we die ?
Perish we in this great city,
None to save and none to pity ?'

IV

" 'Mid the snow and 'mid the hailing,
 Christians, hear the orphan's wailing !
 Ye are bless d with Heaven's plenty,
 While their fare is poor and scanty
  Loud the blast
  Whistles past,
  At your door
  Stand the poor,
There are many in this city,
Few to aid and few to pity !'"

Frank read this little poem with much feeling, and when he closed, Mr Precise arose and walking to his side, laid his hand on his shoulder and after looking down in his face a moment, said

" What is your name, young man ?"

" Frank Hennock, sir "

" Oh, yes, it was so in the letters, I had forgotten," and then Mr P once more read the letters over

" You seem to be a good boy, Frank ! I like you, if you do well and are particular and faithful, I'll do well by you I am very *particular*, you must remember that ? Now, what wages do you want ?"

"I don't know, sir, really, I have a poor mother to take care of!" Here Frank took care that his voice should tremble a lit tle, while his face became still more elongated

"Love your mother, eh? I *knew* you was a good boy You shall have forty dollars a month, commence at six o'clock to morning morning Remember, at six o'clock, exactly"

"I can come to night, sir, if you wish"

"I *said* six o'clock, I don't want you one minute before or after that time I get up at ten minutes before six, I am dress ed in exactly ten minutes, and then I come down and read the morning papers Jenny makes the fire at five You understand me now?"

"Yes sir, I will be here"

As Frank said this, he arose to leave the room, when again Mr P asked

"Have you been to dinner, young man?"

No, sir," replied Frank

"Then stay here till dinner is ready" The elderly gentle man took out his watch, and after glancing at it, said

"Jenny will set the table in precisely eleven minutes I have but two servants one is my cook, the other my house maid"

Then another thought seemed to cross the mind of Mr P "Do you ever drink wine?" he asked of Frank

"No, sir," replied the latter, "it goes against my principles to drink"

"Good boy—very good boy! No small vices—quite neat—I do declare I m in luck," muttered Mr P, and then he asked again

"Do you like to go to church?"

"Oh, yes, sir, I always go when I can"

"What church do you go to?" continued the other

The quick eye of Frank caught sight of a large ornamental prayer book, upon the centre table, and without hesitation he re sponded

"To the Episcopal, sir"

"I o my own church—I have indeed found a treasure con tinued Mr P, and then he said

"Go to the door, Frank, and ring the little bell which hangs there, Jenny will come, and you will bid her show you to the

room next to mine   You will just have time to wash before dinner—I always wash before dinner—you will find soap there of
my own making, very fine old soap it is, too '''

The young man obeyed the order—Jenny came and Frank
shown to the room   As they went up stairs, Frank could n
help admiring the neat figure of Jenny, who was indeed a ve y
pretty girl   The room to which he was shown was like everything in the house, neat, clean, and orderly to an extreme

When the maid opened the door, she paused and said

" This is the room, sir "

" Thank you, thank you kindly, my fair friend," replied Frank,
with a little affectation in his tone , then as he saw that she still
paused, he remarked

" We shall be better acquainted by and by, Miss Jenny "

"La, why you know my name," said the girl , "how did you
find it out ?"

" Our master told it to me "

" *Our* master '" echoed the girl , " why, you aint a going to
come and live here, are you ?"

" Yes , I am his private secretary "

" I don't know what that is," replied the girl , " but I'm so
glad you're coming   I never sees no company , the old cook is
deaf as a post, and I've been *so* lonesome "

The bell from the parlor interrupted the conversation, and
Jenny was obliged to hurry below

" Just the very kind of a place for me , I am like to be appre
ciated all round, above and below stairs," muttered Frank, while
he prepared himself for dinner

CHAPTER VII

———————

STILL another place and a new scene in our metropolis, reader

In Frankfort street, close by Gold street, stands a dingy looking, two story frame house, which has been long known as a " water ing place" and " dance house" for thieves and pickpockets Regular thief soirees were given here, at the date of our story, and very popular among crossmen was Dame Buckley, the hos tess thereof

She prided herself on her English derivation, or rather on her birthright, for she was, like some other of our friends, a lady of the " St Giles" class She gloried in calling her house " The Star and Garter," and boasted oft of the "old country liquor" which she kept on hand The best " mountain dew," the finest " bog poteen," the richest ale and porter in all the States, could be found, she said, in her cellar The *lady*, at the time of the present writing, has found a more central position in the city, where, at " the Rising of the Sun," any reader who is so disposed can find her, and learn if the following portrait be not correct

Madame, or Kate Buckley, as she prefers to be termed, is full five feet ten inches high, the same length of tape would be re quired to pass around her and in shape she very much resembles an exceedingly large sack of wool, girded in the middle and tied with a ruffle at the top With light brown hair, not too thick for comfort in summer weather, eyes rather small, of a bluish grey color, and a face that looks very like the sun rising through a fog bank, she stands in her " native beauty" before you She looks as if " a wee drop of spiritual comfort, taken often," was her doctor s prescription indeed, if we may judge from looks, we can believe that, like the Irish grog shop keeper, she is her own best customer Were you to see her as we have, surrounded by her *peculiar* friends, the flashy crossmen of the town—her thin

nair curled into all kinds of neglige tresses—her flabby ears pen
dant with huge, broad ear rings—a fathom or two of red and
yellow ribbon bound around her head and neck, looking for all
the world like a sailor s idea of a " Moll Wapping " grog shop
sign, you would think her a subject for a moment's study

But to our story   On an evening not much later than that
which chronicles the meeting of the burglar gang at Jack Circle's
establishment, Madame Buckley had a grand soiree at the " Star
and Garter "   Little Charley Cooper and his pal, Big Lize, were
there , but none of the others whom we met at Jack Circle's,
though the entire company was composed of crossmen and their
women

The music was made up of one fiddle scraped by a blind negro,
a tambourine played by a very fat Dutch girl, and a harp touched
not very lightly by " a German travelling artiste," and to the
concord of sound thus produced, many a lively measure was
stepped over the dame's rather greasy floor   Cotillions, fore and
afters, reels, and waltzes were danced , liquor " suffered " some,
and jollity was the order of the night

But while the dancing was going on in the outer room, in an
inner and more private apartment, a still richer scene was occur
ring   It was something like to the fo'lowing sketch —

The hero here, who is displaying his oratorical powers, is none
other than Captain Julian Tobin, one of the finest looking men, and
the most expert pickpocket that walks Broadway, or attends the
crowded places of amusement   Some of our readers may have
seen him for in pleasant weather he   a fond of   n a no

and down the street, displaying a fine figure full six feet in height, well proportioned, a decidedly aristocratic face, generally ornamented with a very neat pair of half whiskers, sometimes with a moustache, which, for convenience sake, is false. He has an eye of dark hazel, piercing and brilliant in expression, features rather sharp, but regular and pleasing, and dresses with genuine taste. He is, indeed, a perfect specimen of a chevalier of the old French school, though his age is near fifty years, no one would suppose him to be over forty. He *was* a French Baron—was disgraced some twenty years since and driven from society in his own country for cheating at cards, he became then a regular gambler, but was so expert in his tricks, that no one would play with him. He next assumed his present profession, and became a " gnof " or pickpocket. Many a " swell " has lost his " dummy " through the skilful agency of Messieur Tobin, and to do the *gentleman* justice, it was ever done neatly and without disturbing or agitating the nerves of the sufferer.

To illustrate the great professional pride of this hero, we must relate a little anecdote. He was detected in a crowd, where a man had just lost his pocket book, or " dummy," and was arrested by a police officer who knew his trade. Taken before Justice Matsell, his first inquiry, in a very bland tone, was

" For vat, Messieur Matsell, ave I been arrest zis time ?'

" For cutting that man's pocket open," replied the magistrate.

" Vel, sare, the offisare ave fiisk me, he ave not found ze skin or ze dummy, eh ?''

" You may have thrown it away, you had better own up, we know you."

" No, by dam, Messieur Matsell, I ave not touch his dummy ! Let me see his pocket—let me see where it has been neeked, sare, if you shall please !''

The mutilated garment was shown to him. One glance at it, and then his former calmness and polite composure forsook him.

" By dam Messieur Matsell, I considare zis one grand onsoolt, one ver grav affront ! By gar, sare, I no neek him ! Ven I shall do a job, I do it up ! I no botch him in zis way—I no neek him, no sare, by dam ! Nevare !''

The pocket had been very awkwardly cut, the slit was ragged and three times larger than was necessary for the felonious abstrac tion Captain Tobin was shocked at such a botching piece of work, and was more indignant than LOCKWOOD would be if an unfashionable garment, or an ill fitting coat was falsely attributed to his establishment

The Justice was convinced that this job had not been done by Captain Tobin, and the ci devant Baron was discharged from custody

The meeting which we were about to describe, was composed of about a dozen and a half of thieves and " knucks," who were listening to a dissertation on the art and glory of their profession, coming from the lips of Captain Tobin

" Ah, shentlemens," said he, at the same time, touching his glass of claret to his lips,—he would drink no other liquor—" Ah, shentlemens, zis is one life of ver grand excitement! You go into a push—you keep one peep open for ze coppare—ze ozzare you keep move 'bout for find ze dummy, eh? Vel, you no shall see ze coppare—you shall feel for ze dummy, or ze skin, you shall sink you 'ave got him, by dam one coppare come look you right in ze ver face! You get very much excite, eh? But, by dam, you no say nossing—you go look for anozzer push, and zen, may be, 'ave ze good luck—touch ze swag, and zen you 'ave make ver much glory, ver much hono*nor*! Ah, it is one bizznasse magnifique! Napoleon ze gran Napoleon, would 'ave make one ver gran gnof, if he try S'pose like me, zat gran sheneral shall 'ave misfortune ven he was young, eh? S pose he lose his rank, he come ze fob on some of ze *nobilitie*, and zey invite him to go to Amerique, as zey did me, he would 'ave been one ver grand captain like me, eh? Yes, by dam! He would 'ave been ze Napoleon of New York!'"

After thus delivering his opinion of Napoleon, Captain Tobin seated himself behind the long table, and with an air of dignity commenced sipping his claret

While he did this, another of the party arose, and a curious looking customer he was Standing exactly six feet three inches high, round shouldered, and withal, a little stooping, Mr John Murphy was anything but a beauty His face was thin and long of the mould usually called ' lantern jawed"—his complexion smoky, his eyes small and dark, his whole appearance

thiefish

He arose, and looking first at Captain Tobin, and then at the rest of the worthies, said

"By Jabers, Cap'n, but it's you that's got the larnint, and I'd rather hear you spake than to patter myself ony day—but I've a bit uv a questin to ax ye'"

"Vel, sare, vat shall it be?" and, as the Frenchman spoke, he looked with a rather contemptuous expression upon the dirty, badly dressed fellow who stood before him

"Why, if ould Boney would 'ave made as good a gnof as yer honer, what would ould Nosey Willington 'ave been if he'd adopted the perfession ' '

"By dam, sare, nevare mention zat man to me' Dam ze man zat wheep ze gran' Napoleon'" The Frenchman emptied his glass now, and with a very ferocious air, grasped the bottle and refilled it

"I beg yer pardon, Cap'n," continued Mr Murphy, "but if you spake uv the one, the other is as sure to come afore ye in yer thinkin box as two crows of the same color, and ye never seed a white one'"

"Blast me if I have'nt' " said "Long Bill," alias William Williams, *Esquire*, another tall, villanous looking dog, with *thief* written by the nand of Nature upon every feature

"An' where was it, Bill that ye come foreninst the crater?" asked John

"Why in ' the Bay' to be sure—there where I seed the red monkeys, and all that '"

"Was it where you married the she nager?"

The brow of Bill, black before, grew darker still at this question, and he replied in a growl

"Better be careful of yer blarney, my cove, or you'll know the game uv fives afore ye die'"

"And by Jabers, Jack Murphy is jist the lad that ud like to be larnt that game by the likes uv you'" cried the Irishman, squaring his immense form into a position for action

The Englishman sprang to his feet, and was about to pitch into Murphy, when Captain Tobin arose very calmly, and stepping between them, in a very quiet tone, said

"Beg your pardon, Messieurs, but zis is ver wrong Zere is no need for fight viz yourselves, ven you must fight, do it viz somebody zat is your enemy S'pose you take one glass of grog, razzare zan fight, eh ? '

" Bloody my eyes, if I cares which '" cried Bill , and with one of his most comical squints, Murphy added

" Divil the bit uv difference ud it make to me, if it wor na for obleegin' the Cap n I'll drink wi ye Bill '"

The two villains at once sent a pale, sickly looking girl, who stood back by the door, out to Ma'am Buckley for a stiff 'ner each, of grog, and the quarrel was settled for the time

While these things were going on within, the " ball" in the outer room was progressing on the Crockett principle, and the thieves, with their *ladies,* were enjoying their share of this world's fun and " nothin' else "

We have given you here but a glimpse at this scene, for the purpose of introducing you to some characters which will here after take prominent parts in our drama, and repay, perchance, the lack of interest which this chapter may possess We have a hard task before us, in following *real life,* instead of imitating some great *predecessors* in foreign cities, and giving a clear scope to fancy , and we shall need the kind indulgence of our readers we were about to say of the *critics* also, but will not, for with them we intend to be as independent as a wood sawyer on a rainy day with a " quarter' in his pocket, asking no favors—wishing none

CHAPTER VIII

———

WELL, Charley, how did you pass the night? Rested sweetly, I hope! You slid off so quietly, that Gus and me didn't even miss you, till we heard that you had gone to look at the pictures!'"

Thus, in a light and careless tone, did Harry Whitmore address Charles Meadows, when they met the morning after the trio had determined to go on a " bender " The meeting occurred just in front of *Pinteux*, and Meadows really looked as if he needed a gin cocktail, or some other reviving beverage He was pale and haggard, his eyes were sunken, and had a blue semi circle be neath them Whitmore looked at him in astonishment

" Why, Charley," said he, " you look as if you'd just been dragged through a sick Frenchman! What is the matter with you, my boy?"

With a dry, husky voice, Meadows replied, as Yankees often do, by asking another question

" Do you think that they ever drug their wine in that place?" said he

" In what place do you mean—in Leonard street?"

" Yes, there where I have passed the night God forgive me for it!"

" Why, what made you think so?"

" Because I only drank three glasses of wine, and it made me as drunk as I could be I have been stupid drunk all night, and awoke just now with such a headache as would make a saint forget his prayers, and set a Millerite to cursing!"

" But you remember you drank brandy before you went in there "

' Only four or five glasses I never was capsized with so little before, I am sure that the wine was drugged "

"No, I don't think Jule ever would allow it, but I can explain the way you got tight so soon   You had been drinking strong brandy, and then, walking in the cold, did not feel it, but your coming into a warm room suddenly, and taking three or four glasses of effervescing champagne, laid you out   I have been served so a hundred times"

"Well, it may be so," sighed Meadows, "this is the first time I ever spent such a night, and in such a place   God grant it may be the last"

"Oh, pshaw!   Why, Charley, I'm sorry to see you so   Let's go in and imbibe a cocktail, you'll feel better after it   By the way, how's your purse this morning?"

"Empty   I gave every cent to a poor unhappy creature who has promised to leave the dreadful life, which from misfortune and necessity she was obliged to lead, and go home to her poor heart broken mother   She has a sister, too, dying of consumption, and now she can see her before she dies"

Harry looked at his companion a moment steadily, then burst out into a hearty laugh

"Do you mean to say," cried he, "that you gave Kate Hall he whole of your money?"

"Yes, every cent   I know it was half yours, but that I will refund"

"And she told you about her sick sister—her heart broken mother, eh?"

"Yes, but why do you smile? why use this tone of levity?"

"Because I did'nt think you could be quite so *green!*"

"I can't understand you, explain if you please!" cried Charles, in a tone of mingled mortification and anger

"Why, Charley, there is no use of crying over spilt milk, but you've been awfully gammoned   Kate Hall has a sister, but she is as bad as herself   The two have been "out" for this ten or twelve years, and the sister has no more the consumption than I have the botts!   As to the broken hearted mother, that was all humbug   You've been most egregiously fooled!"

"Excuse me, *Mister* Whitmore," said Charles, in a stern tone —"I hope that I know enough of nature, not to be deceived quite so easily   I tell you that tears are not to be made to order, and pumped up as you would salt water from a vessel's hold!"

" That's just where you are mistaken, Charley You needn't get mad with me, but as I said before, Kate Hall has most essen tially done you brown ! She promised to quit the life she leads ?"

" Yes, and I, in turn, promised her never to enter a house of that kind again !"

" Well, by Jove, she *was* smart ! She only wanted you to keep clear of her in future I'll bet you 'five hundred dollars that if you'll go there one week from now, you'l' find her, and she will be the jolliest girl in Jule's crowd Will you bet on her ?"

" Yes, I will, sir ! I am not a fool, and I would be one if I was deceived in that way ! I'll bet you five hundred, and when it is won, I'll send it to the poor girl whom you so belie !"

" Well, Charley, you shall, *when* you win it And now for that cocktail "

The two young men entered the beautiful saloon of Pinteux, and doubtless the pretty bar maid of the " Cafe des Mille Co lonnes " suited them to a T with the desired beverage

They came out in a few moments, and Meadows seemed to be in a much better humor Whether this was caused by the spiri tual comfort which he had just taken, or by a smile from the pretty bar ma d, or by some new concession from Harry, we are unable to determine

As they stood in front of the door, Harry said

" You go down town, Charley, do you not ?"

" Yes," replied the other , " I shall breakfast at Bardotte's, and then go to the store "

" Well, we must part then I'm going up town By the way, when shall we meet ?"

" Whenever you please, after business hours "

" Well, say up here, two or three doors above, where I always buy my cigars—where sweet Mary deals out tobacco and smiles nightly "

" At *the pretty cigar girl's,* do you mean ?"

" Yes , have you never been in there ?"

" No , I do not smoke But I have seen her as I passed the window "

" Well, meet me there at six, or half past if it suits you better Mary is a great girl, using the *figurative* sense I've a story to tell you about her some time But you'll be there ?"

" Yes, at six, exactly, for at half past six we take tea at home, and you shall go up to tea with me   I wish you to see my 'Bella, and my mother "

Oh, what a speaking volume there was in the pleasure flash which gleamed from Harry Whitmore's eyes, as he received this invitation   It said more plain than words—"all is in a right train —I am in luck—Satan is helping his own "   But he quietly re sponded

" I shall be most happy   I'll be on the spot, Charley "

Then they separated, the one going down, the other up Broadway

CHAPTER IX

FRANK HENNOCK had been installed two days in his new situation, and in these two days had completely wrapped himself in the good opinion of Mr Precise. And Jenny, the maid, declared him mentally to be "a proper, nice young man, and so 'mazin cute over his books, that an unlarnt body couldn't help a likin' him !'"

It was on the second night of his secretaryship, the hour seven, and at a cosy little tea table sat Mr Precise and his confidential clerk, as he was pleased to term Frank. The coal fire gleamed brightly in its polished grate, the tea urn steamed cheerily, the large astral lamp threw a mellow light over the neat apartment

While all was so comfortable within, the wind whistled through the leafless branches of the tree that stood before the house, as the seaman often hears it pipe amid his rigging, when, with reefed sails and bending spars, his ship dashes and plunges through a storm lashed sea. The sleet came with a harsh and cutting rattle against the closed window blinds, and all the sounds which they could hear, spoke of cold and storm

"It is a bitter night, Francis—a bitter night. It reminds me of what you say in the poem which you read to me," said Mr P., at the same time bidding Jenny, who waited at the tea urn, to place one more lump of sugar in his cup

Frank looked very grave, made a shudder, then looking down at his plate, replied

"Yes, sir, and it e'en a'most kills me to think how the poor people do suffer in such times as this ! I can't eat any more supper now, sir, for you 'bring to memory back the feeling'—no, the scene I mean, which I saw on the very night I wrote that poem A scene where starving, freezing, dying wretches lay in filth and rags and misery all around me ! Oh, sir, I do thank God that I have a home and place, but were I rich, I'd not sit here, **no sir, indeed** I would not!"

"What would you do?" asked Mr P, in a kindly tone

"*Do*, sir? Why, I'd go out and help the poor creatures—I'd carry 'em bread and clothes. There are one thousand persons in one house in this city, and I don't believe there is a fire in the whole house, or even one bed! I saw that on the night when I wrote that poem, sir!"

"*Francis!*" said Mr P, and he raised both his hands, either to express surprise or disbelief "Francis, I cannot believe this! Young man, if you ever deceive me in but one single word, I am done with you for ever!"

Frank crossed his hands upon his breast, and his face wore a look of deep humility and sadness He must have been pained by this insinuation

"I am sorry, sir, if you should doubt me, but if you will go with me this night, I will show you worse scenes than I have related, or you may discharge me in a minute,"

"I will go," quickly said the old gentleman, "yes, I *will* go! Jenny, my thick cloak—my over shoes and woollen tippet Bring them, I'll drink no more tea!"

But upon a second thought, Mr Precise said

"I have drank only *four* cups, I believe Eh, Jenny?"

"*Only* four, sir," replied the maid

"Then, before you go for my things, pour out one more I always drink five—and put two of those lumps of sugar in, Jenny, and, by the way, it seems to me that you've broken them a trifle smaller than I directed"

"May be yes, sir, but I didn't mean to if I did I always try to be very particular," replied the neat little maid

"So you do Very good girl—very good girl! I'll do well by you, if you keep on so"

The maid's pretty blue eyes sparkled as she heard this, and she quickly turned out the cup of tea, and putting in two of the largest lumps of sugar, handed it over to Mr P

"A trifle too full, my dear, a trifle too full," said Mr P, "I never like to have a drop spilt into my saucer"

"I'll be more careful, sir" And again the maid curtseyed and blushed

' Well, now go up stairs and get my things, I'm agoing to walk out "

" Oh, master, do not, please ' Hear how the wind blows and the sleet comes down '"

' That's the very reason I'm going out, child Go and get my things,' replied Mr P , firmly, and then he raised his cup to his lips

Jenny turned to obey, saying at the same time, " I only thought —I was so afeard you'd git a cold "

" A good girl—a very kind, considerate girl '" said her master, when Jenny, carefully closing the door as she always did, had left the room " She'll make some man a good wife ,—neat, tidy, particular, saving, and pretty—very pretty '"

Jenny had paused in the entry, with her ear to the key hole, and of course heard this

" How I would like to be his wife—I do so want to be married ' But I can't get him I wonder if Frank don't feel like gittin mar ried ' I *will* be somebody's wife before long '" These thoughts were murmured as she went up stairs for her master's things

In about a half hour, Mr Precise and Frank were fitted for their tour of inspection, and they started out, Jenny having very carefully loaded her master with everything in the shape of tip pets and comforters which she could prevail on him to wear

The two walked up as far as Broadway, and on the corner they waited for the omnibus which they could hear rattling along over the hard pavement Soon, as it drew near, by the lamplight, they could see its driver wrapped in his oil skin cape and heavy drab over coat, and that he could see them was testified by his up raised hand, and voice almost as sharp as the wind

" Down Broad*way?* Ride—sir, *ride ?*"

A nod of assent from Mr P brought the omnibus close in to the side walk, and our two friends were ensconced inside in a mo ment When they got in, there were but two persons inside, and one of these recognised Frank in a moment He did not, however, see Frank's sign for him to remain unknowing and unknown, but reached out his hand quickly and said

" Ah, ha ' my young frent ' I ver glad for see you '" And then Captain Julian Tobin, looked at Frank's companion At a glance he saw that he was well dressed—he saw also, as his cloak was open, that a gold chain around Mr P 's neck, betokened a watch to be in the fob, and his dark eye sparkled while he gazed

Frank saw that it was too late to deny the acquaintance, and with perfect composure, said

"Good evening Captain Delamere ' I'm glad to see you '"

Captain Julian, shook the young man's hand heartily, then as he shrugged his right shoulder slightly, gave a side glance toward Mr Precise, as much as to say—"introduce me "

Frank at once did so, and Mr Precise thought the Frenchman a very gentlemanly man, both in looks and manners

The other occupant of the " bus" was a woman, and seated in the farthest corner from the light, she seemed to avoid observation She was dressed in deep black A black silk hood was close drawn over her face, and beside this, a thick crape veil of the same color, completely hid her features from view She seemed tall, and even though much muffled up, appeared to have an elegant form

The " bus" now rattled down the street swiftly, but no more passengers got in The night was so cold and stormy, that few, save the necessity driven, or the prowling thief, were abroad

Captain Tobin made himself exceedingly agreeable, and soon, in the course of the conversation, learned the intentions of Frank, and also got an inkling of the " lay" which the latter was on

When the omnibus had got nearly down to Leonard street, the lady in black, as me must term her who sat in the darkest corner, pulled the check string twice, the driver obeyed the sign and drew up at the left side of the street Her sixpence she handed to Frank, who politely offered to pass it forward through the change window to the driver After she got out, Frank, from mere curi osity, glanced through the window to see which way she went As the " bus' drove on, he saw that she had paused before the door of a bowling saloon, the lamps of which were opposite to where she alighted, and seemed to be beckoning or making signs to some one within

" Some *liaison* or other '" muttered he, but at the same moment he pulled the check string, for they were at the corner of Leonard street, as he knew by the bright lights of the CARLTON HOUSE

" You vil get out here, sare ?" said Captain Julian, " Ah, mon Dieu ' but is ver colt ' I shall help you out, sare—wrap you cloak ver tight, eh! I shall help you!" and the polite Frenchman made himself exceedingly busy about his new acquaintance Frank's keen eye had detected the heavy but short steel nippers or scissors which the Captain held in his hand as he assisted Mr Precise, and he knew at once that his master's "thimble" must change pockets

"Halves!" he whispered, as he passed out first, by Captain Fobin

"Oui—to be sure, I nevare sheat my *frents* !" replied the expert pickpocket in the same low tone—then pulling again the cloak of Mr Precise around him, he started to hand him out, but at the moment stumbled and both of them slipped on the icy steps and fell

"You is not hurt, sare, I hope?" said he with an air of great concern, as he helped Mr P up, and then receiving the thanks of the old gentleman, he sprang into the omnibus, crying

"Go on, driver, I, myself, shall pay ze fare!"

And well he might, for, as the stage went on, he drew forward to the light and examined the watch which he had just succeeded in getting, by cutting the gold safety guard

'By dam!" he muttered, in a low gleeful tone—"by dam, I ave make one gran speculatiore ! Zis is one real Londonare, sirteen diamond ! By dam, zey do glis'n ! One hundred seventy five dollare at least for ze timble, fifty more for ze shain ! By dam zis is ver goot speculatione !"

CHAPTER X

———

AFTER Frank and his new master had reached the sidewalk before the Carlton House, the former led the way down Leonard street toward Centre Soon they passed the dark and frowning walls of the gloomy looking " Tombs," wherein, at that moment, was many a heavy heart and burning brain , many a haggard wretch, upon whom the weight of crime was far heavier than all the chains which could be laid upon him

Mr Precise loked up at these high walls, and, as he gazed, said to his companion—

' What is that place ? I did not know that there was such a one in all the town "

" It's the jug, sir," responded Frank

" The jug, Francis ? The what ? I don't understand you !"

" The Tombs, I meant, sir The crossmen always call it the jug "

" The Tombs ? I have heard of 'em often, but I always thought they were some low, dirty jail place—some mean underground cells—not such an immense, castle like building as this "

Mr P paused now, for they were in front of the building, and he looked upon its massive pillars, its dark and heavy front, and a feeling of awe stole over him, as the shade of a rising storm cloud gathers over a sunny meadow

" It is an awful place," said he, and then they went on His guide now kept across Centre, and down Orange street to the Five Points Their approach to the place could easily enough be known by the distant sound of fiddles and tambourines, for on its borders every house serves the double purpose of a brothel and a dance house

The old gentleman drew close up to his young clerk, for these were new sounds that he heard, this wild music, and he began to hear shouts and yells—the laughter of drunken women, and the curses of villanous looking men, who were staggering about very close to him

"Take my hand, Francis—take my hand and keep close to me," said Mr Precise, in a very under tone   "This must be a dreadful low place, isn't there some danger ?"

"No sir, not while I'm along," replied Frank   "I know their ways, you just keep cool, and say nothing, but use your peepers"

"You're a brave, good boy, Francis, but what are peepers ? You use some strange expressions"

"I was using the kind of language which you'll hear to night, sir   Peepers mean *eyes*, but hurry along with me, sir, and don't be afraid, I'll take care of you"

"You're a brave boy—I like you—I'll do well by you, I will!'" murmured the old gentleman, and then he drew closer to Frank, for now they were in the Points, and strange sights, smells, and sounds came to his senses   He gazed with wonder at the long rows of little wooden buildings, their cellars sunk far below the swampy street, and, as he passed them, he gazed upon rooms filled with ill dressed men, and painted, bloated women, who were drinking, dancing, shouting and carousing

Every little while he would mutter, "it's an awful place here—an awful place," and he would shudder and start as the disgusting looking creatures would stare him in the face

As they drew down to the centre, to the point where five streets meet, Frank paused and said—

"I'll show you the soup house first, sir, where a good many of these people get all they ever eat!"

Frank led the way into a nasty looking little place which stood upon the corner before them, and Mr Precise saw a long, narrow counter, before which stood a row of miserable looking creatures, some eating from nasty bowls and tin cups a dark, greasy mess, others with pieces of meat in their hands, still others with glasses filled—not with water

"Stand here in the corner and look on for a little while," said Frank, in a low tone

"I feel sick—I shall vomit if I stay here   Oh, *such* a smell!

Who could eat here let us go '" whispered the old gentleman
But as he had to move aside from the door to get out of the way
of some new comers, Frank drew him to the corner

These new comers were a man and two women, all three Irish ,
and the cloak of Mr Precise contained more cloth than they had
on altogether

" And it's a saxpence we've got, and a bloody good blow out
we'll have uv it," cried the man as he entered , and then turning
to a small pox marked, pale, thin faced, red eyed woman, who
had an old coffee bag for a shawl, he added

" I say, Nance, shall we have some o' the ould divil's broth ?"

" I don't care, Jemmy, so it's sumthin' to eat ? Niver the bit
have I had hould of the day '" replied the woman And then her
female companion added, " An', by me sowl, it's me that can't
brag of bein' ahead ov ye, Nance My ould man, or my ould
divil, has niver come anigh me for a month now, and the childer
be all gone off, too, the snakin' brats "

" Never mind that, *Missis* Haggerty ' I've a saxpence, an it's
my threet now—it is "

As the man said this, he crowded into a place in front of the
counter, and assuming quite a patronising tone and air, cried

" It s a penny 'orth o' broth that I'll have, and I'll have thray
spoons to ate it wid "

" Down with the clink, then," replied one of the dirty looking
fellows behind the counter, and when the Irishman laid down the
penny, he handed over a bowl of the nasty looking scum which he
had called for The three spoons were in it, and each of the trio
seized one, and went to work The bowl contained about a pint
and a half, and it took these creatures about fifteen seconds to
clear it, and the man closed the meal by *licking* the bowl clean,
and handing it back

" An now a wee drap of the crater wudn't hurt us," said he,
again laying down one penny

A glass of very white looking liquor, called by those who drink
it " turpentine gin," was handed over, and the glass was full
The man took about a third at a swallow, then handed it to Nance,
who took her share, and passed it to *Missis* Haggerty for a finish

" An now, *ladies*, what shall we be afther having nixt ' I've
got more money left oe jabers '"

"An it's a smoke 'ud comfort me poor breakin heart!" replied *Missis* Haggerty, and her motion was seconded by Nance

"An it's a smoke we'll all have, so just lind us the loan of thray pipes an' a penny 'orth o' baccy in 'em!"

Three more cents were laid down—three short stemmed, black, clay pipes, that had probably been in a thousand mouths before, were lighted by one of the "clerks" of the establishment, he taking a whiff through each to do so, and handed to the party. They were still obliged to stand before the counter and smoke, for fear they would run away with the pipes, but they were not long in getting through

Handing back their pipes, the *feasted* turned away to give place to others who were coming in

"An' its yerself that's the gintleman, Jemmy!" said the women as they went out, "an' a blessed good time we've had wid ye the night!"

During this scene, Mr Precise had hardly breathed—his eyes were fixed upon the poor creatures before him

"I wouldn't have believed it, he whispered—*five cents*, and they consider this a luxury. What is that black looking stuff made of, Francis?"

"Out of the offals that are thrown from the market, and the scraps of meat and leaves of cabbage and all that which is thrown out from the kitchens in the back alleys, sir. Haven t you seen little children going about the streets with old bags picking up the refuse of the gutters?"

"Yes, and grown people, too!" replied Mr P

"Well, they bring all of that stuff here and sell it!"

"Oh, Heaven! *can* it be! You did tell the truth about the poo people, Francis!"

"Why, sir, you haven't seen the *poor* people yet. The poor people don't come here. They can't afford it!"

"What! Now, Francis, don't tell me stories, you're a good boy, but don't tell me stories," whispered the old gentleman

"We'll see bye and bye, sir, we'll see!" replied Frank, and now let us go from here

They were about to pass out, when again the door opened and Mr Precise drew back from the object which entered, with a shudder

It was an old, white haired man, at least the very few hairs upon his head were long and white   He had no hat on, and the sleet was still laying mixed in with the thin hairs upon his skull   His features were as sharp as bones could be, for the skin seemed to be pasted down upon them, even as would look a skeleton head with cracked parchment stuck upon it   He had no coat, a kind of shirt, made up of a piece of blanket, badly torn, without sleeves, an apology for a pair of what once had been summer trowsers for some sailor—and a pair of old socks made out of a piece of cast away carpeting, formed that old man's dress   Had he not been so dirty he would have been very pale, but he had been laying down in some muddy place, and was carrying about a paper sheet's thickness of it upon him   He might have been seventy or eighty years old—he might not have been over fifty, for poverty makes people grow old very fast

Mr Precise looked at this old man's sunken eyes, they were fairly *encaverned* in his skull, and looked as if daylight could hardly get in to them   He saw this with one hurried glance, and as he drew back with a shudder, he murmured

" My God ' Can all this *be*, in a Christian city '"

The old man drew up to the counter—in a feeble voice which sounded like the dull, dry crash of a rotten limb broken slowly from a tree, he asked of one of the fellows behind the counter,

" Please give me a little of the soup—only a *little*   I ha'n't got no penny, but I'll get one to morrow   I could'nt go out to day, I was sick '"

" Then wait till to morrow for your soup   We don't *trust*, and you knows that '" answered the brute

Tears gathered in the eyes of Mr Precise, he was about to start forward, and one hand was in his pocket, when the old man spoke again   His voice trembled even more than before, and two large tears came out from those sunken eyes, as you may have seen a drop perspire from the edge of a great rock

" I ha'n't had nothin' since the bowl I bought last night, and I'm *so* hungry '" he said, as he pressed his long bony fingers against that part which, among our aldermen, is so apt to be prominent

" I han't got your belly to take care of—clear out '" cried the *thing* who stood behind the counter in a tone more dog like than before The old man made no reply—he gave a kind of long breath, an *attempted* sigh—for he had not strength for a decent one Then as he turned to go away, came a groan,—Oh, how like it was to the sound which I once heard when I bent over the grave of a loved one, and saw the first clod of earth cast upon her coffin It gave back a dull, sickening echo,—how like to that echo was the old man's groan

Mr Precise could no longer stand still, he sprang forward to the side of the old man, the hand which had been in his pocket was withdrawn, and in it was gold—bright yellow gold

"Here, old man, here!" said he, and as he spoke, his voice was choked and husky, and great tears chased each other swiftly down his flushed cheek—"here is money, buy food!"

The old man looked at the gold, then at the offerer, he reached out his bony fingers to clutch it, but then he drew them back and shook his head

"Ha'n't you got a penny?" said he, "that's too much, they'd murder me for it if they knew I was so rich!"

"He is right, sir" chimed in Frank, and even *he*, hardened as the young villain was, wept, but he continued—"the best way to serve him is to give him food and clothes, not money He is old and weak, and the rest would rob him—kill him too, as like as not!"

"Then food he shall have and clothes too—here old man, I've got a warm cloak on, put it over your shoulders!" and Mr Precise was about to give him his cloak, when Frank again stopped him

"Don't do that, sir, it would be torn away from him and carried to a 'fence the moment your back was turned! If you'll go and buy an old suit at a second hand shop they *may* let him keep it, if it isn't worth much!"

Mr Precise looked around at the villanous, haggard, hungry looking set who crowded up to see this scene Their eyes were fixed upon that piece of gold in his hand, and they glared as would caged wolves at a piece of meat, when they were starving

"It'll be dangerous for us to stay here!" whispered Frank "you ought not to have shown so much money We'll take the old man out and get him food in a more decent place!"

But now the whole crowd opened a begging chorus at Mr Pre

cise   "God bless yer honer, an' it's me as hasn't had a bit to ate
for a wake, and the childers nather!" cried one   Then, in ano
ther tone, came an appeal from a hideous, pox marked, one eyed
negro girl, who was so near naked, that the savages of Africa
would have been ashamed of her

"What shall I do—what shall I do!" cried Mr P , as they
crowded in on him, and pushed him back against the wall   He
was for a moment in a very dangerous position—there were two
or three big negroes, regular Five Point thieves, who had crowded
in   Frank saw that they were pressing forward, and with quick
presence of mind, seized the piece of gold and pitched it to the
end of the room farthest from the door

"There, take it and divide it," he cried

With howls and curses at each other, the whole crowd rushed
after the gold, pitching and tumbling over each other in their
eagerness to get hold of the money—each one striving, fighting
to get it for him or herself

"Now—quick, out we go!" said Frank, and he raised the old
man up in his arms and rushed for the door   It was a light
weight—that bundle of skin tied together bones   His master
followed, and as he got outside he heard shrieks, curses, and heavy
blows within   As a pack of hounds fight over a hare—as they
tear each other in the attempt to get a bite at the victim, so were
these poor wretches fighting over that gold

"Oh ! God of mercy, is this real, or a dream ?" groaned Mr
Precise, when he found himself outside in the wind and sleet once
more, and then he paused to listen to the terrible sounds within

"Don't stop, sir—don't stop, or some of 'em will be 'spotting'
you!   Let us keep ahead—I ll take him to a decent grocery,"
said Frank   Rushing along across the open space in the centre
of "the Points," he paused at the door of a little shop at the
corner of Anthony street, and said

"We'll go in here , but where do you live, old man ?"

"I don't live anywhere now !" replied the poor old creature ,
"I did live in the brewery, but I couldn't pay my board, and they
turned me out !"

"Well, you shall have a place there , I'll see the agent in a
minute   Come in here, sir," and Frank beckoned to his master
as he set the old man on his feet again , "come in here, we'll get

him a fit out, and then we'll go to the *brewery!* There's the place where *some* poor folks live !"

They went into the shop, which was half filled with whites and negroes, nearly all poor and ragged, some well dressed wenches, others, villanous looking creatures Some, were buying liquor—others wood—still others, food

"Now, sir, we'll make our purchases," said Frank "I'll take my arm's full, and you shall pay for 'em"

First, Frank took a dozen small sticks of wood from a large pile, which was corded up on one side These were about six inches long, were perhaps an inch square—then he called for a string of onions—a piece of salt pork, a nasty looking piece they gave him, too, one which would weigh four or five pounds—a loaf of bread—a candle—and a card of matches Then he told the clerk to hand the old man one of a pile of second hand blankets which lay inside of the bar. This was done

"Now, sir," said he to his master, "we will go Just pay the bill, and mind don't show any *gold* again"

"How much is it?" asked Mr P of the clerk

"Let's see—wood, twelve sticks, three cents, meat, ten cents, onions, three cents, blanket, a quarter dollar, bread, a penny forty two cents, all total, sir Throw off the odd two cents, sir, you've bought so much!" replied the fellow behind the counter, who seemed much more decent than the other

Mr Precise stared at the man with a gaze of astonishment for a moment

"Havn't you made a mistake?" said he, "it's very little"

"No, I guess not Oh! yes, I did, there's the candle and matches, another cent, that's all"

Mr Peter Precise liked to be particular, and so he took out of his vest pocket a little change—he counted out four ten cent pieces and three cents

"There's the amount," said he Then turning to Frank, he asked

"Where now—where shall we go?"

"To the brewery, sir, to find a boarding place for the old man"

At this moment they heard a faint sob—the old man had been eating some of the bread, and had got strength enough to weep, and as he stood there with the blanket around him, the tears came

6

again from some place in back of those deep set eyes, and he sobbed.

"It tastes so good, I can't help it, but it tastes *so* good!" said he in broken accents, and then Mr Precise wept once more.

"Let us go now, it is getting latish," urged Frank.

"I wonder what time it is?" said his master, and then, when he felt for his watch, he discovered its loss.

"Well, I do declare!" he cried. "Why, how can this be? My watch is gone, Francis!"

"Is it, sir?" asked the young man earnestly, then looking at the fob and feeling if it were there or not, he added in a tone of astonishment—

"Why, so it is! I was afraid that them fellows in the soup shop were crowding a little too close on you."

"Do you think they took it there?"

"Oh, yes, sir. Them were all thieves, except one or two that were *low* beggars! This old man here wouldn't steal, but all of them darkies are thieves by profession."

"Oh, *my*! What a place this is! Who *could* have dreamed it! I gave two hundred and thirty four dollars for that watch and chain—they asked two hundred and thirty five, but they discounted one dollar because I paid them in city bills. And I never felt them take it, how strange!"

"No, sir, not so strange. They do up such things amazing neat."

"Well they *do*!" and Mr P said this feelingly, as if he felt fully convicted of the fact.

"And now for the brewery. Come along, old man—come along, Mr Precise. We'll go now where *poor* folks live!"

The three went out into the street. It was astonishing how much difference a half loaf of bread had made in the old man. Why, he scarcely tottered at all as he led the way—he took steps almost as long as Frank did—and they were quick glad steps. The poor fellow had at last met with a ray of summer's sunlight in his clouded winter—he had actually found a *friend*!

They went along the street until they came to a large brick building, once used as a distillery, now known as *the* "brewery." Into an alley which leads down one side of it, a narrow, horridly smelling little sink of about two hundred feet long, known by the name of " *Murderer's lane,*" the old man led them   About half way down this, he paused and pointing down into a dark place, that seemed to yawn up, like a very mouth of darkness, at their feet, said

" There's where I boarded, afore they turned me out '"

" Let us go down and see the place ' ' said Frank, and then he took one of the candles which he had bought and stepping into a door way, ignited a match by rubbing it against the wall, and lighted his candle   Then he came out, and stepped down into the cellar, which doorless, lay before them   The old man fol lowed—then Mr Precise

As they stepped into the *hole*, we cannot honestly call it any thing else, Mr Precise gazed around in speechless wonder   The tallow candle gave but a dim light, yet it was enough for him to see the contents of that room

In one corner lay a heap, apparently, of rags, but at the sound of voices, and the glare of light, the heap moved, and a woman, a pale, haggard looking wretch, whose uncombed, dirty and mat ted hair fell down upon bony naked shoulders, raised up and gazed with a wild, inquiring stare upon the party   As she did so four children of different sizes, raised up and gazed too—and the poor things looked even more wan and wretched than she, and their faces wore an expression of mingled fright and wonder

Mr Precise looked in another corner—there he saw eight or ten—blacks and whites, raise from a perfect knot   They had hardly any clothes—and had been sleeping close, to keep warm for a lot of old coffee bags, and some pieces of carpet was all that covered them   He shuddered—was about to speak, when a low, moaning groan was heard from another corner still

He turned, and he saw a woman lying upon the bare earth— her face was all broken out in red blotches—two children laid be side her—one was very red in the face, like herself—the other was deathly pale—still its face looked as if birds had been peck ing at it , or, as if some eating, chemical acid, had been dropped over it   The three had not enough clothing on to conceal their thin, fleshless limbs—they had no bed—not even a stone for a pillow

" My God ' worse and worse '   Good woman are you sick ?" cried Mr P , as he rushed up to her side

" Yes," said she faintly, " an' I belave one o' the childers has died, for the poor crater is cold, an' it won't spake "

" Oh, heaven, so it is '" cried Mr. P., as he felt its thin wrist, and found that its pulse was still, its hand ice cold   " What was the matter ?"

" I don't know," replied the woman, and she seemed hardly able to breathe—" we've all been sick for a wake, and maybe the poor thing has died uv nothin' to ate '"

' Nothing to eat, and haven't you had a doctor either ?"

" No, sir, we nivir had as much as a smithereen to pay one, and nivir a one could we git here widout it, and I was too wake afore I know'd it to go to the hospital '"

Frank looked down intently, for a moment, upon the woman and her dead babe, and then started back, pale with fear and horror

" Oh, my God, sir '" he cried, " let's go from here—" she's got the small pox, see it's broken out all over her ' Let's go, every moment is a damp of death to us '"

" No—never will I leave such misery till I can relieve it—never '"

" You will catch the disease, sir, you will die '"

" I care not, if I die in doing my duty ' God will take care of any one that tries to relieve such wretchedness as this '" replied Mr. P., and tears streamed down his cheeks in torrents, and fell, like the holy rain of sympathy, upon that sick woman's form

" Well, sir, what shall we do ? Let us do all we can and go from here '"

" I'll tell you what ' Do you run for a doctor first, and then go and buy wood and food, and clothes, and everything for these miserable creatures ' Oh, God, can this be a *Christian* town '"

" Well, sir, I'll go '" cried Frank, apparently glad to get out of that atmosphere, " but it's dangerous for you to stay here ' You've got money with you '"

" Well, take it with *you*—I don't go from here till I see a change in things ' No, no ' Thank God, I've got money, and now I know what to do with it   There's a pocket book in my back coat pocket, Francis—it has five hundred and eleven dollars in city bills in it, take it out '"

Frank felt in the pocket—it was the work of a second for him, entirely unobserved, to slip the "dummy" into his own pocket, while he pretended to feel for it, then, in a tone of surprise, he cried

"Why, sir, there isn't no pocket book here, them fellows in the soup house must have got that too !"

"The old gentleman felt for it himself—then passed his hand into all his pockets Of course his search was vain

"Well, I *never* !" he exclaimed—"this is horrible But I've two eagles left—here they are, loose in my pocket, take them Francis, and if they don't go far enough, I've a warm coat on, my boy, I'll sell it, yes, and look there, look there ! See them naked creatures shiver !"

Frank took the money and hurried out, and now the old man who had come in with them, looked Mr P in the face

"Mayn't I make a fire, sir ? Mayn't I make a fire out of my wood ?" said he in tones stronger than he yet had used

"Yes, old man, yes !' and as Mr P looked around, he saw the little fire place No sign of there ever having been a fire there, could be seen, the walls were wet, the floor was the same, and filthy, too filthy for description was the whole place

The old man carried his little bundle of wood to the fire place, the sticks were so small that they were easily lighted by a single match, which he rubbed against one of them He only lighted four, for the old man was economical, but they blazed up and showed a brighter light in the apartment And then, an old man, a *very* old one, more thin and haggard, if possible, than the one we have described, crept on his bones—I cannot truly call them hands and knees—through the filth to the fire He crawled close up to it, and reached out his skeleton hands to warm them There was no blood there, why needed he to warm dry skin and bones ? Perhaps there was a little marrow left in them, which he would thaw He had *nothing* on save an old ragged shirt, no other clothing And, as he lay stretched out, he looked at the pile of onions and meat which the other old man had set down beside him, and, though he said no word, his look asked all that misery ever uttered But, as a miser clings to his gold, so did the first old man hug his treasure Where, thought he, or when will I ever get so much again

But Mr Precise saw the looks of both, and he said

"Share with him, share with them *all*, old man! You shall have more, yes, plenty more!"

The old man seemed to do it unwillingly, but he gave the other an onion, it was eaten, skin, root and all, in an instant

"Give him more, then go around and give the rest some!" said Mr P

The old man obeyed, and it was strange to see how the naked, haggard wretches clutched the food—how they crushed it between their tremulous jaws, and then glared around to see if there was not more The string of onions didn't go far among seventeen persons, for this was the number in that hole, and, besides, the sick woman and her living child were too ill to be hungry—they could not eat

"Give them the meat—cook that and give it to them," said the old gentleman

But they did not wait to have it cooked, they crowded around the fire, and, like wolves, tore it to shreds, and gulped it down unchewed It was lean, nasty, dark looking meat, but it seemed to slide right easily down their gaunt necks

"Put on all the wood, we will have more soon!" cried Mr P and he rubbed his hands together with an expression of pleasure, at the thought that this misery should so soon be relieved

And then he walked to and fro across the damp place, but when his eye fell upon the poor woman who was so sick, he saw her shivering with the cold He took his large warm cloak from his back, and laid it over her Never had that cloak covered such a sight before—a dead child, its dying sister, their mother in the same situation

The doctor came, and Frank was with him, bearing his arms full of food and old clothes, and behind him came two negroes, carrying wood and other things

"Good boy—good boy, you've been quick!" murmured the old gentleman "And now, doctor do what you can for these poor creatures I will pay all expenses!"

The physician—a little, fat, round faced, round bellied man, who looked the reverse of Shakspeare's apothecary—bent down over the woman, gazed at her a moment, then shook his head in a very ominous, or rather a meaning way

"It's but little use, I think she's too far gone! They may do something for her in the hospital Better send for a cart, and have her and the live one carried there If the other hadn't died of this, it would have been worth *five* to the students for a subject But it's worth nothing now!"

"What! do they ever buy these poor dead creatures?"

"Oh, bless your soul, yes sir! A most always, they very seldom bury folks that die here, they can always get something for 'em, if they don't die of *this!*"

"Oh God, is it possible! Who could have believed it!"

"Have you been up stairs sir, yet? I've got several cases up there, but they don t pay me much!" said the doctor

"Up stairs!" repeated Mr Precise "What, is there more misery like this here! How many poor creatures live here?"

"All told, I think about eleven hundred!"

Mr Precise did not speak, he actually gasped with surprise

While all this was going on, Frank had been at work trying to make an equal division of the stores which he had brought The wretches seemed grateful for the food and clothes, but many of them grumbled now because no *gin* had come with the presents Such is human gratitude, and this is not the only application where the adage fits, "the more you give to some, the more they want"

But others were more grateful And blessings were asked upon the head of their new benefactor

In a few moments after the doctor had told Mr P the number of beings in that cavern of poverty and death, the latter recovered from his surprise enough to speak

"I'll believe you," said he, "I'll believe anything *now!* Send for a carriage, and have that poor woman and her child taken to the hospital, and have the other buried, decently buried! See to this, and send your bill to me"

"Thank you for your patronage, sir, but I can't get a carriage for her No driver would take her from here I can get a hand cart, and some fellows here that have had *it*, to draw her!"

"Well, well—anything to make her more comfortable—do what you please Ah, Frank, you re a good boy! You told the truth! Yes, I'll do well by you, I will, but I m not rich enough now I'm agoing into business again"

" You *are*, sir ?"

" Yes, yes, I've got to make more money, for now I know what to do with it "

" You are *too* good, sir '"

" Oh, no, I'm not half good enough But let us go around and see more of this "

" Oh, sir, you've seen enough for to night We'll come ano her time "

" Well, Francis, you are my guide for this night * I am your elder, yet I will act under your direction "

" Thank you, sir You'll not lose by it But you've been rather unfortunate, losing so much to night "

" Oh, no I have lost money—I've lost a good, regular going watch, but I've gained a knowledge which will give me more pleasure than aught else I could gain I know what to do with my money—I know what to do with all I can make hereafter ' I've often been a little scared, Francis, at the thought of death, and felt right anxious to know how I could work my passage into Heaven, but now I've learned it God *will* repay one who devotes all the latter part of a not ill spent life to relieving such misery as this Yes, in future I live for the poor—for these wretched, miserable creatures '"

" Well, sir, as I said before, you are only too good ' But we'll go from here now You've made a happy set here "

" Yes, thank God, yes '" replied Mr P , as with brimming eyes he turned to gaze upon those whom he had relieved, and then he turned to go

" Stop a minute, Francis," said he, " did you tell that doctor where *we* lived ?"

" Oh ' yes, sir, and that sort of men never forget the address of any one that they can raise change from "

" Well, then, I'll go with you, but let us go home now, I'm sick of this '"

" We'll go sir, but I'd like to have you stop in to Pete's, and see a little of high life on the Points "

" Where is Pete's ? Who is he ?"

---

* We actually are afraid that some of our readers will doubt that this description of misery in the FIVE POINTS is true but we only ask them to go to the places which we describe and see for themselves

"He is one of the upper-ten of darky dom, sir!"

"Well, where you please, I'll go *any* where now!"

Leaving the doctor to attend the sick family, and the rest enjoying a treat, rich as it was unexpected, the two now retraced their steps through "Murderer's alley," and then across to one of the streets beyond the triangular square, which centres the sink of misery. Up this they walked but a few steps, and paused at a low door, where the inward passage was downward.

Mr. P. heard the sound of music within, he saw a large negro standing at the door, apparently to guard it.

"Is this the place?" asked he.

"Yes, sir," said Frank, "come in, sir!"

But the huge Ethiopian planted himself before the entrance, saying

"A shillin' afore you comes in yah, Massa!"

Mr. P. felt in his pockets; no shilling was there, but this lack of "*tin*" made no difference, for Frank pushed forward, saying

"You know me, Sam, I'm on the *cross* !"

Mr. P. wondered at this strange expression, and still more was he surprised to see the negro step aside and admit them without another word.

And yet wider opened he his eyes, when he stepped within. He saw *a* sight! Not less than two hundred negroes, of every shade, from the light, mellow cheeked quadroon, down to the coal black, were there. Some were dancing to music made by a fiddle, a tambourine, and an exceedingly ancient looking guitar all of them played with more strength than sweetness, and speaking of this latter, the atmosphere was not tinctured with too much of it. Those who were dancing, of course, kept neck and neck with the music, to do so, it was impossible not to sweat some, and the odor raised therefrom was less agreeable than some of the perfumes which GORAUD has invented.

Mr. P. saw that those who were not dancing, were seated around the room, some smoking, others chewing "the weed," still others drinking. The last were supplied by a tall, rather good looking fellow, behind the bar—whose wife, a very handsome quadroon, was dancing on the floor.

As soon as Mr. P. entered, a middle sized man—of course a

colored one, came forward to Frank, with a broad grin that **showed** at least four inches' width of ivory

" Ah, how d'ye, Masta Frank ? Glad to see you down **yan,** you an dat nice lookin gemplem !"

" This is Pete Williams, the proprietor of this establishment !" said Frank to his master

The latter bowed, while Pete, bending almost to the sanded floor, said

" Berry glad to see you, Masta ! De honor ob your 'quaintance be appreciate by me, I shure you ! Walk aroun an' see de ladies ! '

Pete was very well dressed, his plaid waistcoat did look rather flashy, and his very rich cravat was too showy for good taste , but he looked better than any of his company

" Come back and see green eyed Andy ! He's a natural curiosity !" said Frank—" he can palm a die , or slip the loaded ones, better than anybody in this village !"

" I don't understand what you mean," replied Mr Precise— " but I'll go where you wish now and see what is to be seen !"

Frank led the way into a back room, where a crowd of darkies were standing before a little table, upon which lay a " sweat cloth," or a square piece of oil cloth, marked thus —

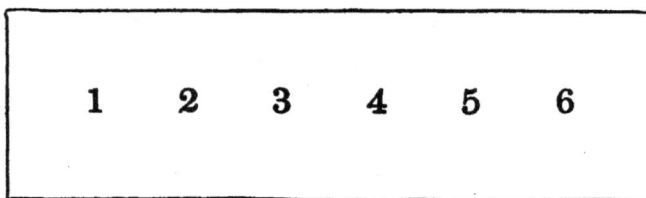

1	2	3	4	5	6

Behind this sat an old negro, whose very few hairs were not black, and as each of those who stood in front laid down their bets, he shook up his three dice, and laying them out upon the table, took up all the money which had been placed upon the figures not similar in number to those which he threw For in stance bets were made upon the one, four, three, and five, he would be sure to turn up his dice two, **five, and six,** so that one bet only could win, while he took those that lost

" Why do you call him ' green eyed Andy ?' " asked Mr Precise, after looking some time intently at the game ; **and also at** the negro who shook the dice

" Because he always wears green specks, sir, I believe   That is all the reason I know   His real name is Andrew "

" This is gambling, isn't it ?"

" Yes, sir   On a *small* scale, not anything large   The ' bank' here is worth six or seven dollars, not more '"

" Well, do let us go, there is nothing here which interests *me* '" said Mr P , evidently quite disgusted

The twain now turned to the outer room, where they found that the general dancing had ceased a moment, for a " juba dancer" was on the floor   He was a young mulatto, and to the liveliest tune which " the band" could play, he was " laying it down," in a dance, where every step in the hornpipe, fling, reel, &c , was brought in , double shuffles, heel and toe tappers, in and out winders, pigeon wings, heel crackers , and, then, to close up, the richest step of all that ever was danced, the winding blade was footed

Mr Precise paused, and the first expression of admiration which had passed his lips, came then

" What wonderful agility '" said he—" what astonishing quick ness , why, the fellow seems to be made up of hair springs, he hardly touches the floor '"

But even this ceased, and Mr P got out once more amid the wind and sleet of the stormy night, and he and Frank went home

Some of our readers may have seen what they thought was poverty, walking in our streets , they have often seen such sights as are pictured here,

but they have not seen real misery, nor can they, until they visit the spot which we have only *commenced* describing   We have given but one picture in the " brewery" when we have seen an hundred such, and must yet paint them for you , and many a dark hole is there in the " Five Points," which we will yet lay before you

CHAPTER XI

READER, stand in the cloak of invisibility with me, and let your imagination paint for you a beautiful boudoir, a lady's chosen sanctum   Richly furnished, its curtains, carpets, ottomans, all of the softest and most voluptuous colors, each little article of *bijouterie* which a wealthy and a tasty woman would desire, is there   Pictures, rare and costly, hang upon the curtained walls, the marble tables are covered with books and periodicals   And through a door in its rear can be seen a chamber furnished full as well   Everything in view betokens wealth used with taste, ele gance not marred by anything illy contrasted

From the windows, however, you may see something which *would* contrast with this, you can see a field of bones—a spot where many a grey and ancient stone tells the last incident in man's history, when and where he whose dust is beneath, died. Yes, a grave yard lies almost beneath those w ndows, and a tall church steeple towers so high that its shadows can fall upon the velvet curtains of the window whence you gaze   One would think it a singular coincidence—but many a premature death, many a broken heart has been caused by deeds done in that house, and while we look down upon the grassy tombs, we can speak of ruin wrought quite feelingly   You will not understand me, un less I write more plainly   On the floor next beneath that where is the boudoir, which we have been looking at, is a gambling *hell* —a place where more than one young man has been ruined, where the first blow has been struck which brought disgrace upon him, broken hearts and desolation unto them that loved him

Yes, one of the most fashionable and one of the vilest of all the hells in Gotham, overlooks a grave yard

If, as people once did think, the spirits of the dead can arise at the midnight hour, they could find plenty of company by simply crossing a narrow street, and they could see all of the passions displayed which are ever felt in the human breast They could see the drama, comedy, and tragedy of nature, they could see alternate hope and despair, anger and calmness, fear and courage, they could see men trying to drown conscience in the burning water of fire they could see villains rob villains, they could see genteel stealing and wholesale robbery, not of money only, but of virtue, principle, aye, of honor, and all that makes the soul of man precious to itself

We speak of what we have seen, for many a sickening hour have we spent in studying these scenes We have gone within these hells—we have marked looks, expressions, and characters, until the book is as one committed to memory, a memory which holdeth all that it has gained

Why Mr Henry Carlton, the gambler, should have selected so *fitting* a spot for his hell, we know not, we only know what too many young men of our city are aware of—that it is *there*

But we were describing a lady's boudoir, and though it was so very near the grave yard, it looked as if it had been fitted for love and happiness, as if never a thought of death or sorrow should enter there

In this room see a lady She is alone In her hand she holds a letter, and a variety of expressions come and go upon her beautiful face while she reads it She is pretty, yes, she is more—is *handsome* Her face possesses intellectual beauty, her brow is high and fair, dark blue eyes, glossy brown hair, delicate lashes to shade her large soft eyes, and a face sweetly oval in form, a figure tall and perfectly proportioned, delicately small hands, with jeweled fingers, a tiny foot slippered in satin, finishes our brief outline of her appearance

After reading the letter which she held in her hand, her face beamed with a pleasant smile She kissed the paper over and over, then placed it in her throbbing bosom

" Dear, dear Charles," she murmured, " were it death, a thousand deaths to love thee, yet would I be thine Thou alone of all the millions who tread this ever changing earth, wert fitted to make me happy Why we did not meet when we were young and I was free, I cannot divine nor why a good Heaven sends not congenial spirits together upon the earth, as soon as they are born '

Then she arose from the ottoman where she had been half reclining, and drawing one of the worked chairs closer to a side table whereon lay writing materials, she again murmured

" I must answer his dear letter—yes, I will meet him as he wishes I could deny no request of *his* "

She drew a perfumed sheet of note paper from a drawer, and in a neat, beautiful hand, soon filled its snow white pages Then carefully was it folded and sealed

After this she rang a little silver bell by her side The outer door opened in a moment, and a middle aged, fine looking mulatto woman entered

" Did you ring, mistress ?" she asked

" Yes, Eliza , take this note to *him* !"

The girl answered only with a look of intelligence—took up the note and left the apartment In a moment, however, she returned

" Mr Sam Selden is in the passage, and wishes to know if you can be seen, madam !" said she

" Yes," replied the lady , " you can tell him to enter and then, Eliza, hurry away with that note Tell no one where you are going, and be prudent , it would be worse than death to have my love for *him* known '"

" Fear not, my lady, I never will betray you I love you too well for that "

" You are a good, honest, sweet girl, Eliza You never shall lose by your faithfulness to me "

The girl left the room once more, and the lady seated herself on an ottoman, in a position of studied carelessness—in a way which best displayed the beauty of her figure, and where the rosy light through a crimson curtain would fall richest upon her cheek

The next instant a low tap was heard upon the door

Her voice was very sweet when she cried, " come in, ' and her smile exceedingly bright, as a well dressed gentleman, not much over her own age, entered He was a little over the middle height, very well proportioned in figure , had a piercingly bright eye of jetty black, deep set under a rather heavy and frowning brow , hair and beard of glossy silkiness, dark as night when the storm is, and the moon and stars are not   A heavy moustache helped to contrast a very fine set of teeth, which, in smiling, as he met the lady, he took particular pains to show, and his rather pale face looked paler still for the same contrast   His dress was tastefully fashionable and very rich, it fitted his genteel figure perfectly, in fact, Lockwood's establishment never turned out a better suit, and one could almost swear to the " Dubois cut " of his beautiful frock, his manner, as he entered the apartment, was graceful and easy

" I am glad to see you Mr Selden," said the lady, " are you well to day ?"

" Quite so, I thank you, madame   I need not ask you the question, you look charmingly this morning   I never saw you look so well "

" Ah, sir, you are ever fond of flattery, but if I do look well, it is because I am in fine spirits   I feel *so* happy to day '"

" Why I thought to find you dull, your husband is absent are not married ladies ever sad when their lords are not near ?"

" Some may be," replied the lady, in a careless tone, and then as the thought came over her that Mr S was her husband's bo som friend, she added   " You forget that he is to come home by this evening's boat   He wrote me so, three days ago "

" Yes, yet he will not be here   I received a letter from him this morning, informing me that he could not come before next week "

" Indeed '" said the lady, in a tone of surprise, while a but half hidden ray of pleasure lighted her eye

" Yes, madame," continued Mr S , " and in his letter he sent a bank note of five hundred dollars for you   Here it is "

" He is ever very kind, but I did not need money   He left me a thousand dollars only ten days ago, and I have not spent half of it yet   The lady sighed as she spoke of her husband's goodness, and her face seemed a shade paler while she crushed up the bill in her fingers

Perhaps she was thinking of that sin which even then was lurking in her heart, she was thinking perchance of the wrong which she had meditated upon his rights and honor—even already might have consummated

This scene and these characters we must now leave for a little time, to return to it and them, of course, in another chapter, for among all of our pictures, the one they are connected with is the wildest and darkest—one which brings in all the strange, fierce passions of the human heart—Love, Hate, Jealousy, Revenge, MURDER

7

CHAPTER XII

Not far from the centre of our city, in a street which runs pa
rallel with Broadway, stands a fine looking three story brick house,
with green window blinds in front, which, for some reason or
other, are never thrown open   It is a very neat, plain fronted
house , no name is on the door , its number, however, is promi
nent

Speaking of its front, reminds us here to say that there is an
other entrance from a back street   A high fenced alley leads
into a back yard in the rear of this dwelling, and many a muffled
form, close veiled and trembling with fear and excitement, has
hurried through that narrow little lane, and entered that singular
house   We will not yet say what this house is—we will let it
tell its own story , but we will say that there is not only one,
but more than a hundred of its kind in the city

There always seems to be a kind of mystery about it   No
noise or disturbance is ever heard within its walls , it is quiet,
still as a convent or a Church   Yet strange monks and nuns
would those make who go there

The very next door neighbor knows not who dwells in this
house , the servants of it will not speak to his servants nor ur
fold the secret, which is often and vainly sought for   When twi
light darkens, and night comes on, many a man is seen to enter,
yet they, too, seem to wear a studied disguise—sometimes veiled
females are seen to go in at the front door, though nearly all of
the visitors to that dwelling, have the singular habit of entering
by the alley

We will go in through the second story window, reader , yes,
through blinds and all, in our *fancy*, and look at one who is there
seated and who but a moment before had come in to the house
by the back alley   As he entered the house, he had met a lady,

a middle aged, good looking one was she, and in a low tone had whispered, "send to Mary, No —— Broadway, and tell her that I *must* speak to her a moment, before she dresses for her usual duties."

The hour was about five, but as at the season when we write (the early part of January, 1841) darkness comes early, on this occasion it was twilight.

The gentleman, after giving this order, ascended to the second story front room, which we are now to look at. It was furnished in a magnificent style, red velvet cushions to each chair and sofa, crimson satin curtains to the windows, many fine paintings were hung upon its lofty walls, all of them, however, of the French school, voluptuous—too much so for description here. In an alcove, at one end of this large parlor, the curtains of a bed could be seen, so that this room could be doubly used as a chamber and a parlor. Upon a table of variegated marble, in the centre of the room, stood a large globe astral lamp, which threw a warm, rich light over it. A cheerful fire—coal of course, gleamed in the grate, and a piano, flanked by a guitar, set off the end of the room opposite to that which contained the alcove.

And now for one look at the gentleman. He was tall, well formed, elegantly dressed, in that truly tasty style which men of birth and wealth ever adopt.

His age, apparently, was fifty, perhaps not over forty years, his complexion florid and healthful, his features rather fine, yet so formed as to denote a character of great sensuality. And yet, with all, there was an expression of refinement even in his sensuality, he looked very like what we would have deemed the famous Earl of Buckingham to have been at the same age.

Seating himself before the fire, he took some letters from his pocket, and selecting one which had already been opened, he commenced reading it, and as he did so, soliloquized.

"By the hint which she gives here, I fear that both her and myself are in rather a bad scrape. I like the girl, I would not wish to see her disgraced—nor can I save her, for I am married. I wish that she had known it from the first, it would not now be so hard to break it to her. I once thought that interest alone influenced her, but now it seems that love for me must have led her where she is.

"If her hint be true, what can I do   There is but one thing   I have heard of a wretch in Greenwich street, one MADAME SITSTILL, who makes a trade of *murder*, who, for a few dollars, will bind herself to destroy *one* life , in doing so often takes *two*   If the worst comes to the worst, I will send Mary to her

'The girl writes prettily   Little did I think when six months agone, I met thee, Mary Sheffield, all would have occurred, which has   By accident I saw thee, where hundreds before and since have seen thee—standing in thy smiles behind a counter where the ' weed' is stored in every shape "

The gentleman folded up the letter, placed it in his pocket, then looked at his watch

"It is time she was here," he muttered impatiently, "it is not far—not more than six or seven blocks to her employer's shop , the servant must have been tardy in delivering my message , I know that Mary would hasten to me if she knew that I was here "

Then again he paused, sighed heavily, and gazed steadily into the fire as if he were reading a lesson from the burning coals , a lesson which would learn him that the fire of the human passions, like the flame before him, would destroy the very fuel on which it feeds

Whatever may have been his reflections, they were disturbed by a low tap at the door, and without awaiting an answer, the one who touched it entered   It was a female—a young, *beautiful* creature   She could not have been over seventeen or eighteen, judging from her sweet and girlish face , yet a full, perfect bust, such an one as Canova would have given his left eye to have copied, and a figure perfect in all its proportions, were hers   We cannot well describe her, but just fancy one of the prettiest blondes that ever poet idealized or painter pictured, and Mary Sheffield stands before you

She hurried across the room to the gentleman's side, and clasping her rounded arms about his neck, impressed a warm kiss upon his brow, then while a tear stole down either cheek, murmured

"I am *so* glad, my Albert, to see you once more   Three long days of anxiety have passed since I wrote you   I heard not one word , and much as I have trusted, I began to fear that you, whom I so love, had deceived me !"

"No, my Mary," replied the gentleman "I have been absent,

up the river to Albany, on business I only received your letter an hour since, and have ever since been cogitating upon its con tents Have you really cause for the hint which it contains of your situation ?"

The young girl blushed deeply, hung down her head, and in a low tone replied

"But too much, sir Oh! how unhappy I have been for the last week, but I will be so no more You will marry me now?"

"Mary, I cannot yet I have reasons which I dare not now reveal Yet at this time there is a bar between us which will delay our marriage"

'Oh! dear, dear Albert, there must be no bar! No! In a few short weeks my situation will be but too apparent, I shall be turned from my place! I am so well known to every young man in the city, that my name and shame will be bruited everywhere! Oh! death, anything, were better than this!'"

"Speak not so, my Mary, I will not so desert you All that I can do, I will You shall never say that I deserted you, and left you to the wintry blasts of scorn I cannot yet take you as my wife, but you shall have a house to live in I will visit you often, and ——"

The girl arose from his knee, where, in childlike fondness, she had seated herself, and while her blue eye flashed with feeling and her red lip quivered, she interrupted him

"You would make me your regular favorite—you would more debase me than you have! Oh, Albert, I have fallen, sinned far worse, far more than Mary the Magdalen! yet will I not do this No Make me now your wife, as long since you said you would Do it, if you are a *man!*'"

"Mary, I cannot I will support you, at all expense, and at all risks, I will preserve you from the danger of your present situation'

"Albert, do I understand you? Is not one of the risks at which you hint, the loss of my life? To comply with that to which you allude, must I not be a murderess?"

"No Use not such harsh terms, my dear It is not murder! Mrs Sitstill, to whom I would send you, is a kind woman, a very useful one to society Many a girl from the highest grades of our aristocracy thanks her now, that her name is free from stain"

"Yes," cried Mary, "yes—with a pale cheek, a sunken eye, a broken constitution, and more, far more, the burning fire of con science, that gnawing worm which never dies—such may live, but must I be one! Albert Shirley, you could have married me ere this if you would, but," and the girl shuddered now, "I be gin to fear that you are like some of the rest of your sex of whom I have heard. You have, like the bee, taken the honey from the flower, it may droop, fade, and wither, while you buzz on in search of another"

"Mary, you wrong me Within two weeks I will satisfy you"

"Albert, dare I trust you! And yet I must, for where can I find redress or aid I am a helpless female, if my disgrace should become known, the world would whip me forth into the wil derness of vice, it would scorn, detest, drive me mad with con tempt and insult He who stole from me my purity—who led me aside with false promises and honeyed words, from the pathway of the good, might still bask in the world's sunshine, while I, more sinned against than sinning, would be driven, naked of fame and honor, into the gloomy night of helpless misery and despair! Think you that it is their fault, that hundreds of poor females— young, beautiful creatures—haunt our streets nightly to pursue their revolting, self sickening calling? No, sir, it is not! But who would raise a hand to aid them? Not even a wall will echo back an answer They are not worth a breath or a sound!'"

With astonishment Mr Shirley had listened to the rapidly uttered remarks of his strange and beautiful companion, and they were too true for him to answer

She did not await a response But while her cheek was yet red with excitement, and her eyes were flashing through her tears, she turned to leave the room

"Stay, Mary, stay a moment When shall I see you again?"

"I know not, Albert Never, if you intend still to trifle with me I can die alone, as well as with you, if I am not to be your wife!"

"Say that you will spend Sunday afternoon here with me, I may have good news by that time"

"I will, Albert, but I must hurry away now It is already time that I was in the shop I must go and stand amid the filthy fumes of smoke—to hear coarse jests made upon my person—to be but a sign to attract coxcombs and dandies to my employer's counter "

" Poor girl, this shall not long be so !" said the gentleman, in tones where kindness and pity were blended

" Indeed it shall not—it cannot ! I will not live so ! Sooner, far, would I at once spring into that unknown, which the wicked dread, and even the righteous cannot gaze upon without a tremor "

And then they parted The poor girl, muffled closely in her cloak and veil, first hurried from the house by the back alley , then, ten or twelve minutes after, the gentleman too stole forth from this singular establishment

CHAPTER XIII

———

READERS, we hope you have not forgotten our poor little sewing girl   Though she is of a class that seems entirely to be forgotten by the good people of this city, we claim an exemption for her   The poor creature cannot possibly last long   One winter of destitution—one bitter season of toil amid starvation and wretchedness, must sicken her   If she sickens, she dies, for then she cannot labor   Were she, scorning the opinions of that world which scorns her poverty, to cast herself into the hot house of vice, she might get along very well as regards mere food and clothes, for a winter or two, but let us rather hope to see her freeze, starve, *die* in misery, with purity still in her soul, than to yield to the fatal step which would engulf all that is precious and beautiful in her character

The reader will remember that all of the events in this number of our work are embraced in the space of only four or five days, so that they need not expect to see Angelina again until our next number, when they will find her *changed*, but pure even as the crushed snow drop, or the lily torn from its stem, fading upon a dark and frozen soil

And do not think that she is a creation of our fancy   We have no need of " creations" in this work, the reality is ever before us   Vice, poverty, crime, and wretchedness, are not only every day words, but every day sights among us   And whose fault is it?   We cannot say, but let it be found out.

There are thousands of sewing girls here, whose characters and sufferings are but duplicates of those we attribute to poor Angelina   But leaving her, we will introduce you to another character   She is of that better class of " the fallen," known in Paris as the *grisettes*, here, by no particular name

MARIA DELORAINE,

Must have some evident occupation, some apparent business, or she could not live in the respectable family where she does, for they, with that spirit of know everything ativeness, which is our national character, would be sure to inquire how she got her money—how she managed to dress so neatly and well

Therefore Maria has chosen the easy and beautiful trade of an embroiderer or worsted worker, and in this occupation spends all of her leisure hours We say *leisure* hours, because she had another business than this, one which we will not now name, but which, in the course of our work, shall tell its own story

She boarded with one Mrs Windeman, a respectable widow lady, one of that " class which has seen better days, ' but was *reduced,* as she was ever saying, to the unfortunate necessity of keeping a boarding house 'Twas dreadful, but it *was,* and though she and her seven maiden daughters, descending from the age of thirty to about twenty, spoke often of the faded glory of former days, when they "rode in Pa's carriage and lived up town," they had right hard work to keep up the thread bare appearance of former gentility

They lived in a large three story brick house in Greenwich street, and kept nearly every class of boarders which they could pick up But these they managed to classify, as well in rooms and price, as at the table, for a few medical students from the South were mixed up with the daughters at the extreme head of the table when at meals Below these sat four or five clerks, as the next most genteel, and still farther down, sat some rough looking mechanics—hard working men—who paid their board regularly dealt honestly, but who, of course, could not be so *genteel* as the rest, though some of the others seldom found it convenient to " settle up " with Mrs W

Maria never was seen at the table   She had a parlor and bed-room on the second floor , to this her food was carried, and seldom did she make her appearance elsewhere in the house   She pass ed, with Mrs W , as an orphan, who had a small income from a legacy left her, and worked at her embroidery for the rest of her means   She saw but little company, and even Mrs W and her daughters acknowledged that they were *real* gentlemen who came to see her

At the time when we introduce her to our reader, she was alone in her parlor, working at a piece of embroidery destined for a chair back, and though she worked steadily, it did not seem as if her mind was at her employment for she kept ever and anon starting up, looking around and acting as if she expected a visitor

Nor did it occur that she should be disappointed   The little Irish servant girl, Rosa, came into the room, and said

" There's a gintleman below, as wants to see you ma'am— here's a bit o' paper that he guv me, wid his name on't, may be !"

" Yes, it is he ," replied Maria, looking at the card, " ask Mr Whitmore to come up !"

The servant disappeared and soon Mr Whitmore, our old friend, made his entree

"Ah, Maria, I am very glad to see you—you look so exceedingly well that I've no occasion to ask after your health !" said he in a familiar tone, at the same time imprinting a kiss upon her cheek, which blushed not at the liberty

" You are well too, I see, Harry   It is long since I have seen you   You do not visit No ' 355' very often now   Mrs I must miss so good a customer as you !" said the young lady

" I *have* been rather steady of late, I must acknowledge , but I shall make amends by and by   Does she keep up her select soirees yet—those chosen parties, limited to *ten* ?"

" Yes, I was there but a few evenings ago   But I received a note from you to day, Harry, informing me that you would be here at this hour, and that you wished to see me on business What do you wish ?"

" Why, I would like to have you to pass as my sister, with a new acquaintance of mine, a young lady, and also with her brother "

" What is the object ?"

" Oh, a mere whim of mine, my dear girl, a mere fancy I want her to come here and visit you, and you to go to see her a few times "

" Were she to come here and ask for a sister of your name, the folks down stairs would open their eyes There is a difference between the name of Deloraine and Whitmore "

" That's very true, my dear, didn't think of that But it can be worked better yet You shall meet her at Madame I 's, there is a greater appearance of fashion and wealth there, and they will act as they are directed The darkie in livery at the door, the elegant furniture, and the fashionable arrangement of the house will be of great advantage to my plan I can always let you know when she is to call, and when she asks for Miss Maria Whitmore, you can of course be the *she* "

" Yes, but what is your aim ?"

" Why Maria, if you will have the truth, I wish to make her my wife without committing matrimony according to the rules and forms prescribed by law Do you understand me "

" Yes, you wish to ruin her—to bring her also into the fearful ranks of the fallen Harry Whitmore I thought that you had made enough victims, more than you wish to answer for, already "

" Oh, don't go to moralizing, Maria, for heaven's sake !"

" No,' replied the girl bitterly—" no, I am not one now to moralize, I know that, but, Harry, this is some poor innocent girl, for whose moral murder you are now laying a deliberate snare "

" I'll tell you what she is, Maria She is a pert, forward chit, that is always condemning those who have made a slip, says that the prison is a sight too good for them, and all that ! She has some beauty, and is fool enough, I think, to like me some, though I have seen her but twice I've already told her that I had a sweet sister named Maria, and she is anxious to make the acquaintance "

" I had rather you would pick out some other accomplice !"

" I know none either so good looking or so perfectly lady like as you, Maria You can make a hundred dollars by carrying on this affair "

We know not whether the hundred dollars, or the flattery

caused the girl to be less firm in her resistance to his desire, but she replied

"It's very hard to refuse you anything, Harry, and if you will promise on your word of honor not to do anything which can get me into trouble, I'll consent"

"Of course I'll promise that, and now for arranging the first meeting I'm to see her again this evening, and to morrow I'll send you a note or see you and say when she will pay Miss Whit more a visit You must remember to say a great deal about your dear, *dear* brother, how good he is to you, and all that"

"You need not fear, sir When I assume a character, I always sustain it"

"Very well, Maria, I'll leave all to your good sense And, by the way, while I think of it, here is a *fifty* You may need some pocket change"

"You had better see Mrs I and give her a caution, so that there can be no suspicion raised"

"I will, as I go up the street And now, my good friend, I'll bid you good evening!'"

"Good evening, sir"

Again Maria Deloraine was alone She was a very pretty girl, and as Harry had said, exceedingly lady like in her man ners She was tall, well formed, of a very fair, clear complexion, with black glossy hair, a fine brow, eye lashes that drooped en tirely over her large dark eyes, and could hide them as she looked down at her work Regular features—a pouting, most kissable pair of lips, and a sweetly dimpled chin, were also hers Though there was much voluptuousness in her appearance, it was mingled with an air of refinement, which made her doubly dangerous She was dressed very plain and neatly, as all women may safely do, who have beauty It is on y ugliness or deformity that requires artificial aid to improve upon it

When Harry Whitmore had left the room, she resumed her work again, and as she stitched away, she murmured out her thoughts in soliloquy

"So—another flower must be torn and transplanted from the garden of purity to the fields of infamy and death And I—I the once pure—must aid in this dark deed But why should I pause, or think it wrong I am here—misery loves company"

CHAPTER XIV

I say, Cap'n, let's be hoff on a new lay that I've ad my peep ers on for a month o' Sundays "

Thus cried little Charley Cooper to Captain Julian Tobin, on the second Sunday night that occurred in our story Charley, Big Lize, the French Captain, and a new friend to us, but an old one of theirs, called " the Stutterer," were all who were present at this time in old Ma'am Buckley's little back room

As " the Stutterer " is a new character, and rather an important one, we will give his daguerreotype

He is of the medium size, not far from forty years of age, is about five feet seven inches high, has dark eyes and hair, the lat ter curling and worn long He dresses very well, but rather flashily, has a dark complexion, frowns when speaking, especially when stuttering badly, which he does when he gets very excited He has the bad habit of swearing a great deal, and once or twice a year takes a trip over to England to see how his friends get along there

But back again to the subject Captain Tobin heard the pro position of little Charley, and taking out a very handsome watch, the identical one which he had *borrowed* of Mr Precise, he glanced at it and replied

" Vere is ze lay—vat shall be ze speculatione, eh ?"

" The Dutch dance house," replied Charley   " There's a lot o' swells as has got to goin' there lately to dance with the Dutch g'hals, and we might do up a job or two of a night, that 'ud pay right fair "

" Vel, ve shall see, ver soon—direcklee Zere is an engage ment zat I expect in some sree or four minute, zen I will go an see vat is out "

"Wh who d'ye 'spect, Cap cap'n ?" asked the Stutterer

"Zat dam lawyare, Messieur Tarhound, he is employ to for me some dam leetle dirty shob, an I must wait for see him till it is eight o'clock,"

"I'll just t tell you wh what it is, Cap'n, it's my private ho pinion, purty d—d hopenly hexpressed, that th that Tarhound is a devilish mean r r rascal He'd steal from a *thief !*"

The Captain was about to reply, when the very individual al luded to verified the old adage—"speak of the devil and he's sure to appear"—by walking in

He was a little over the medium height, well formed, dressed shabby genteel—had dark hazel eyes, straight black hair, worn long over his ears, as if to hide some mark there His face had a kind of *sheneyish* expression, in which avarice, cunning, coward ice, and licentiousness were all so mixed together that they could not be separated Although he vegetated under the name of *C Aggrippa Tarhound, Esquire,* the legal gentleman had no par ticular office, nor hung he out "a shingle" anywhere His clients were generally to be found in or about the edges of the "Points," except when he could get hold of some poor woman or green countryman, whose sorrowful faces as they approached the "Tombs," showed them to be in trouble, and then, if by either personating himself or by *assuming* the *name* of some better known lawyer, he could get a fee out of them, he would do it, *of course* We have a pleasant anecdote or two concerning this interesting haracter, which we will work in hereafter—one especially re arding a "will" and his first debut in Jersey, which is immea surably *rich* He is known only as one of *the* "Tombs lawyers," and as he stands at the head of his peculiar grade, we give him a place in our romance

When he entered the room and saw the company which we have described, he made a low, cringing bow to each, and, in a kind of fawning tone, said

"I'm very glad to see you, *gentlemen ,* glad to see you, *Miss* Eliza, *very* "

"Sorry I can't return the compliment Next to a copper, a lawyer is what I hates the worst, 'specially a poor 'un "

Tarhound's brow, red and liquor stained before, grew a little purpleish at this, but the Captain interfered, and said

"Nevare mind ze lady, sare, she is ver fond of speak in **ze** sarcastique, but we shall talk of ze biznasse   Vat 'ave you do for zem dam boys, eh ?"

"Got a hearing—get 'em out in the morning, Captain Straw bail, and all that   It'll cost *something*, though "

' How great deal ?"

"About a double X, for paying the bail and my fees "

"I shall give you ze monee   But, Messieur Tarhound, if ze dam leetle boys be not go free before noon to morrow, I shall give you one case again nevare "

"Don't fear, sir   I d have 'em out if old Matsell himself was to examine them "

"Ah, dam zat Messieur Matsell, if he was deat, zen would ze gnof 'ave one g and shubilee—one ver fine holiday !" said the French Captain, and then he asked

"Who shall 'ave ze honore of examine ze little boys ?"

' Old Deserve, to be sure, and I can stuff him with anything Why, he thinks I m one of the best lawyers at the bar !"

" Then it's my hopinion th that he can be most b b blastedly s st stuffed," said the Stutterer, quietly, while Big Lize asked

"Wh 's the kids in for, old fuddle cap ?"

" I don't like your complimentary terms, Miss Eliza," replied T , "but I'll answer the question   The youngsters are in for till tapping   A Froglander grocery keeper caught one of 'em with his hands in the money till, his pall didn't keep his peepers open '

"The bigger fool he   Will they have to visit the Island ?"

"No, not while C Aggrippa Tarhound is retained for them   I never let my clients go there if they fork up handsomely "

"C ceptin' when you gets dr drunk on the money and f f forget th the case t till they're sentenced, as you d did with Sal Snow, th the Micky Riley g'hal "

"I wasn't drunk, Mr H , I was only *sick*," replied the lawyer, quite indignant at the Stutterer's insinuation

"Vel, sare, it is not mattare now, zeie is you twenty dollare, tell zem dam leetle rascale boys zat zey must not get grab any more, or by dam I will let zem go to ze island or to ze devile, yes, by *dam*, I will !"

The lawyer liked his company very well, but he had sense

enough to see that they didn't like him, therefore he made his exit

'Now, Sharlee, I vil go viz you on zat ozzare lay, but we do not want many of ze boys, eh?' said Captain Tobin to little Charley

"No," replied the pickpocket "Lize will pal for me, the Stutterer shall pal for you Lize is the best bulk that a file ever knucked after, and we'll go there for an hour, and then come home and take a peep at the swag we both 'ave lifted

"Vel, sare, *tramp* is ze word" And with this the worthies bent their way to Elizabeth street near Grand, where is still to be seen one of *the* sights in Gotham Separating, and keeping on the shady sides of the streets, the select party of four started for their field of labor

But of the doings here—of the treat enjoyed by our pickpocket friends—and the funny swag which they raised out of the Frog lander coves—we will tell the reader in *Part Second*, which will also follow up the histories—comic, tragic, and mellow dram attic —of each character in the past pages, and bring in several new ones, especially of that class termed the cod fish aristocracy

We intend to give, if we live long enough, a perfect daguerreo type of this great city, offending none save those who deserve it, and neither shrinking from, nor fearing to expose *them* fully Our next number will follow in a very few days, and some rich illus trations for it are in course of preparation In the mean time the following engraving will show that we keep a bright

LOOK-OUT ABROAD

A GLOSSARY

OF FLASH TERMS AND SLANG LANGUAGE USED IN THIS WORK

———

Autem divers " Pickpockets in a Church

A 'round " Taking a cruise about town, or going on a spree, is called taking a " round "

A " look out " Keeping a watch, to see if others are coming, &c

A " Skin " A purse

" *Ace of Spades* " A widow

" *Bantered* " To dare one, to defy them, is to banter

" *Bender* " To go upon a spree, get drunk, and raise a muss, is to go on a bender

" *Buck* " An assistant to a cheating hack driver

" *Bung nipper* " A cut purse

" *Bog poteen* " Irish bog smoked whisky

" *Blarney* " An Irishman's small talk

" *Bus* " Diminutive of omnibus, a common abbreviation

" *Blow out* " A feast, or a spree

" *Cribbeys* " Blind alleys, dark narrow ways There are lots of them in the " Five Points '

" *Covey* " A common term for a fellow

" *Chum* " A comrade—friend, used by women and thieves to designate their companions

" *Crib* " A thief house , a " fencing crib," is a place where stolen goods are bought or hidden

" *Chuck* " A term of endearment used among loose people

' *Crossmen* " The professional term for thieves

" *Cracksmen* " Burglars

" *Cross* " To be " on the cross, ' is to be dishonest

" *Cutwater* " Used generally to designate the nose

" *Cracking a Crib* " Breaking into a house

" *Caffers* " Men who have been transported to Botany Bay from England, and have escaped

" *Cracked* " Broken

8

" *Cratei* " The crater—liquor

" *Coppers* " Officers of the police , also termed " pigs," " nabs," &c

" *Cut* " To leave—to " cut and run," is to make a dash and run away

" *Courtesan* ' Woman of ill fame

" *Curtain lecture* " Refer to Mrs Caudle

" *Cl nk* " Clink or chink , money

" *Dan* " An impudent sinner

' *Dunderhead* " A stupid dun

' *Dummy* " A pocketbook

" *Duds* " Clothes

" *Dark lantern* " A thief's glim or light, made so as to shut out the light when not needed

" *Dust* " Slang term for money "Out of dust," is to be lacking change

" *Dub* " A pick lock or master key To go " on the dub," is to go on a thieving expedition

" *File* " An assistant to a pickpocket

' *Fawney* " A ring

' *Fastner* " A warrant

' *Fence* " A place where stolen goods are bought or hidden

" *Flash* " The language of thieves

" *Fat* " Rich ' *Fat cull* " a rich fellow

" *Froglander* " A Dutchman

Frisk " To search, or to take from

" *Glaze* " A window

" *Glisten* " A term used by thieves for diamonds

" *Gold thimble* ' A gold watch

" *Gospel shop* " A Church

" *Gold finch* " A man with plenty of money about him

" *Glim* " A light, or lantern

' *Gnof* " Pronounced *gonof*, a gipsy, and slang term for pickpocket

" *Hays* " The name of our venerable High Constable, used as a warning among thieves, to cut and run

" *Jug* " The prison

" *Timmy* " A crowbar

" *Jugged* " Imprisoned

" *Kicking the bucket* " To die

" *Knuck* " Another term for a pickpocket

" *Kid* " A young or little thief

" *Lushy* " Drunk   Lush, is liquor

" *Limbo* " A prison

" *Lifting* " Stealing

" *Lark* " A cockney's name for a spree

" *Lay* " A place or plan, where and how a theft can be committed

" *Muss* " A difficulty, or quarrel

" *Maul* " To beat

" *Mauley* " The hand

' *Muck-worm* " A miser

" *Mountain dew* " Scotch whisky

" *Nab* " An officer or constable

" *Noozed* " Married or hanged

" *Noddy* " A fool

" *Nob* " A gentleman or man of rank

" *Nymphs of the Pave* " Courtesans

" *Nick* " To cut a pocket and abstract its contents

" *Panel thief* " A woman who entices a man to her house, and there has him robbed

" *Plea at the bar* " Taking a drink

" *Pal* " An assistant to a thief

" *Peepers* " Eyes

" *Peach* " To tell

" *Prigged* " Stole

" *Patter* " To talk

" *Push* " " A push," used by pickpockets to designate a crowd

" *Prancer* " A horse

" *Swell* " A gentleman

" *Square* " Honest   To live on the square, is to quit thieving

" *Spree* " A drunken frolic

" *Sporting man* " Genteel term for a gambler

" *Sponge* " A hanger on, who imbibes all that he can get, and pays for nothing

" *Scot* " The bill

" *Sparkish* " Gay, dashing

" *Sheney* " A Jew

" *Snudge* " A thief who hides under the bed

" *Snakesman* " A small man or boy, used by burglars to push through a window or small hole in a house which they break into

" *Spunk* " Courage, derived from the original Yankee

" *Spooney* " A coward

" *Swag* " Plunder or booty

" *Salt water vegetables* " Oysters and clams

" *Swig* " A drink of liquor

" *Stars* " The police of New York are designated by a brass star on their breast

" *Stumps* " Legs

" *Swell-head* " A bloated drunkard

" *Spot* " To spot is to recognise—to mark

" *Stalling ken* " Place of reception for stolen goods

" *Screw* " A key   " Screwsman ," a key maker

" *Tramp* " To walk   To go on the tramp, is to start off on a thieving expedition

" *Thimble* " A watch

" *Tip* " To give   " Tip us your mauley ," give us your hand

" *Toby-lay* " The Highway

" *Whiff* " A puff of smoke

" *Wipe* " A handkerchief

www.ingramcontent.com/pod-product-compliance
Lightning Source LLC
LaVergne TN
LVHW081347060426
835508LV00017B/1450